THE LIVING BUDDHA

THE LIVING BUDDHA

BUDDHA

AN INTERPRETIVE BIOGRAPHY

Daisaku Ikeda

Translated by Burton Watson

MIDDLEWAY

PRESS

Published by Middleway Press
A division of the SGI-USA
606 Wilshire Blvd., Santa Monica, CA 90401

© 1973, 1976 by Daisaku Ikeda
© 2008 Soka Gakkai

ISBN 978-0-9779245-2-3

Cover and interior design by Gopa & Ted2, Inc.

This book originally appeared in Japanese under the title
Watakushi no Shakuson-kan (My View of Shakyamuni),
published by Bungei Shunju, Tokyo, 1973.

Library of Congress Cataloging-in-Publication Data

Ikeda, Daisaku.
  [Watakushi no Shakuson kan. English]
  The living Buddha : an interpretive biography / by Daisaku Ikeda ;
translated by Burton Watson.
      p. cm. — (The Soka Gakkai history of Buddhism series)
  Includes bibliographical references and index.
  ISBN 978-0-9779245-2-3 (alk. paper)
  1. Gautama Buddha. 2. Religious biography—India. I. Title.
  BQ886.I3813 2008
  294.3'63—dc22
  [B]
                                              2008038569

23 22 21 20 19   4 5 6 7 8

CONTENTS

PREFACE TO THE
ENGLISH EDITION

Shakyamuni was a man who lived some twenty-five hundred years ago in central northern India and who earnestly and untiringly sought to discover the nature of the dharma, or Law, the eternal principles of truth that transcend time and place. He was a thinker of giant proportions who, for the sake of people in ages to come, persisted in his efforts to discover the source of creation and to free human existence from all impediments.

If we, in this present age, were to try to imagine the sort of person Shakyamuni Buddha was, what portrait would emerge? This was the spirit of rather naïve interest, curiosity, and in a sense audacity that led to the writing of this book.

But to construct a picture of Shakyamuni Buddha, one first needs certain materials—historical facts, accurate dates, sources whose reliability is above question—and such materials are, let me note at the outset, regrettably scarce. This is due in part to the fact that the Buddha lived so long ago and in part to the lack of interest in the keeping of historical records that is characteristic of ancient Indian society. But whatever the cause, it renders exceedingly difficult the task of arriving at an accurate picture of the Buddha. At the same time, it makes it possible, and even necessary, for the writer to exercise his imagination to a considerable degree. In this sense, in spite of the great gap in time that separates Shakyamuni Buddha and myself, I think my personal experiences and religious practice have allowed me to achieve a certain feeling for him as an individual. That is why I titled the original Japanese version of this work *Watakushi no Shakuson-kan* [My View of Shakyamuni] and why the subtitle of the English edition is *An Interpretive Biography*. It is my firm conviction that one can seek to discover and understand another human individual only through the medium of one's own identity as a human being, and it is on this premise that I have attempted to transcend the barrier of time and approach the man we call the Buddha. In this respect, my portrait of him, rather than being drawn strictly from bibliographical sources, is no doubt strongly colored by the image that I have formed in my mind of him as the leader of a religious organization. For the subjectivity of this approach, I can only beg my readers' indulgence.

In this connection, it may be well to note that the Buddhist religion is interested primarily in the question of whether a person realizes within himself the dharma, or principles of eternal truth. For this reason, it is less important, from the religious point of view, to inquire what were the specific words and acts of Shakyamuni Buddha as a historical personage than to discover the nature of the dharma that he attained and to ask if other people can attain it as well. The portrait of a man who has attained the dharma—this is the true Shakyamuni Buddha, and it is he whom we wish to know. If this book is read in light of these particular characteristics of the Buddhist religion, and if it serves in some small measure as a spiritual bridge between the East and the West, then my hopes as an author will have been more than gratified.

In closing, I would like to express my deep appreciation to Professor Burton Watson for the time and effort that he has expended in preparing the English version of this work.

Since 1976, when this English edition first appeared, it has been translated and published in at least eighteen languages. As its author, I am immensely pleased that it has thus won a readership extending throughout the world. The publication of this paperback edition responds to the requests of many readers. It is my sincere hope that those striving to create a better society will find this volume helpful in understanding the life of Asia's foremost teacher of human wisdom.

Daisaku Ikeda

TRANSLATOR'S NOTE

As indicated by Daisaku Ikeda in his Preface to the English Edition, the Japanese work from which this was adapted is titled *Watakushi no Shakuson-kan* [My View of Shakyamuni], *Shakuson* being the common Japanese designation for Shakyamuni Buddha. The original work was cast in the form of a dialogue between Mr. Ikeda and one of his associates, but with the author's permission I have, for purposes of smoother reading, recast it in straight narrative form, taking care, of course, to preserve all the factual and speculative material of the original.

Sanskrit and Pali personal names, place names, and technical terms have been introduced in the text in the romanized form that seems most suitable for English readers, without the elaborate diacritical markings demanded by strict Indology.

One point touched upon by Mr. Ikeda in his Preface perhaps deserves special emphasis here for the sake of Western readers. Religions like Judaism, Christianity, and Islam lay great stress upon certain unique historical events or personages and, as a consequence, are vitally concerned with questions of historicity. Buddhism, however, emphasizes the dharma, or body of religious truth, rather than the particular time, place, or person by whom it was preached.

Mr. Ikeda is the dynamic president of the Soka Gakkai International, a lay organization of Nichiren Buddhists. As the spiritual leader of the Soka Gakkai International's millions of adherents in Japan and its growing worldwide membership, he is intensely interested in discovering whatever can be known about Shakyamuni Buddha, the historical founder of Buddhism. But if, as a result of the regrettable paucity of reliable sources, his account of Shakyamuni necessarily includes much surmise and conjecture, this in no way affects the validity of Buddhist teachings. What is important, as Mr. Ikeda himself notes, is not the distinction between historical truth and legend in the accounts of Shakyamuni's life but the degree to which both fact and legend embody the timeless truths of Buddhism and are meaningful to us today.

THE YOUNG SHAKYAMUNI

1

SHAKYAMUNI

Any Asian person hearing this name will invariably think of Buddhism, for Shakyamuni was the founder of that great world religion. But who was this remarkable man, when and where did he live, and what were the circumstances under which he began the preaching of a new faith? These are some of the questions that I want to pursue in the pages that follow.

I have in my mind an image of what sort of person he must have been—a man who, no matter how pressed to choose between one philosophical proposition or another, never forgot how to smile; a sage who, at times with an air of aloofness, at times with an air of pride, and at other times silently and serenely, pursued his own way unperturbed, a way founded upon principles that were engraved on his heart. It is this image of Shakyamuni that I hope to present here.

He was a man who taught neither in terms of any strict or compelling logic nor impassioned dogma, a man who commanded no vast system of philosophy capable of overturning mountains. Rather he was a man who, in almost astonishingly plain and unaffected language, employing anecdotes and analogies that could be comprehended by anyone, sought to awaken in each individual the spirit that dwells in the inner being of all people. By this I do not wish to suggest, however, that Shakyamuni possessed no philosophy at all. When he speaks in his unassuming way to humankind, one catches within the clear and simple words echoes from another realm, that of the truly enlightened man who has contended with and overcome darkness in himself and attained the final resolution of truth.

This is my personal view of Shakyamuni. It is this Shakyamuni, one among many who have searched for the Way, whom I have so long admired and to whom I have felt myself drawn. It is this Shakyamuni, rather than some vainly elevated and apotheosized founder of a religion, whom I want to describe.

Here I have tried to sketch in a few words my image of Shakyamuni as a man. But when we attempt to move beyond this bare outline and ascertain the concrete facts of his life and teachings, we find ourselves confronted by a lamentable dearth of accurate biographical and historical information. In fact, on the basis of the sources that have been handed down, it is all but impossible to reconstruct with certainty the life and personality of this man who lived more than two thousand years ago. In addition, because he was a great religious leader, his disciples and followers in later ages have tended, in their zeal, to exalt and deify him, and a mass of legendary material has accrued about his name that serves only to obscure further the few facts that are known about him.

To begin with, it is difficult even to establish the exact period of his lifetime. The people of ancient India, where Shakyamuni lived, were far less interested in keeping records of historical events or the mundane shifts and changes in human society than they were in seeking to discover the eternal truths that lay behind these daily happenings in the phenomenal world. Even in the case of a figure of such prime interest and importance as Shakyamuni, although they took care to preserve and hand down his thought and religious teachings, they left no precise biographical record concerning the man himself. The typical Indian attitude toward time has been described as casual.

But in another sense, it is this cultural attitude of indifference to time and refusal to be bound by it, this temperament that seeks some stationary point from which to probe into the essence behind the endlessly changing cycles of one's environment, that has given rise to the kind of profound philosophy and religion represented by Buddhism.

The Indian people, it would appear, are by nature markedly philosophical and meditative. Both Buddhism and the philosophy of Brahmanism that preceded it excel in speculative thought and have attained a strikingly high level of philosophical development, probably the highest in the world at the time of their inception. Thus, although India may be an exasperation to anyone in search of historical or biographical data, it is a country that holds endless fascination for the student of philosophy and religious thought. It is most important at this point to understand this fundamental temperament of the Indian people, for it will help to throw light upon some of the problems that will be encountered when we come to an examination of the teachings of Buddhism.

I have stressed at the outset the paucity of reliable data on the life of Shakyamuni, but this does not mean that no sources whatsoever exist. There are, in fact, several biographies of him, notably *Praising the Buddha's Deeds* by Ashvaghosha, the famous Indian poet of the first or second century. But these works were not composed or committed to writing until centuries after Shakyamuni's death, and they appear to contain a fairly large admixture of pure legend.

The proper approach, I believe, is not to attempt to sort out and discard the legendary elements but to consider how and why such legends may have come into being. In this way, I feel, we can arrive at something approaching the truth. In addition, the sutras, or sacred scriptures, that preserve the teachings of Shakyamuni often contain descriptive passages that permit us to determine at least in outline what sort of person he was.

Because of the lack of accurate historical information, there is no agreement among scholars today concerning the exact dates when Shakyamuni lived, though they are generally of the opinion that he lived sometime in the sixth or fifth century BCE. Let us leave this problem of dating aside and focus our attention upon what can be known about the life and personality of the founder of the Buddhist religion.

SHAKYAMUNI'S NAMES

We may begin with a consideration of his various names. It is generally accepted that Shakyamuni was the son of the ruler of a small kingdom headed by members of the Shakya tribe or clan. Shakuson, the name by which he is customarily known in Japan, is abbreviated from the Japanese form of the Chinese version of the Sanskrit title *Shakyamuni Bhagavat*, which means literally "Sage of the Shakyas, the World-Honored One," an appropriately respectful designation for the founder of a great religion.

In addition, from early times in India he was called the Buddha, from which the term *Buddhism* derives, and he is customarily known by this name in South and Southeast Asia and the countries of the West. The word *Buddha* in Sanskrit means "enlightened one" or "one enlightened to the eternal and ultimate truth." There is a strong tendency in Buddhist writings, however, to employ the term *Buddha* to refer not only to Shakyamuni but to any being who embodies the ultimate ideals of the Buddhist faith. Some scholars claim that it was never intended as a proper name.

In early scriptures, as well as in Sri Lanka, Thailand, Indonesia, and other countries where the Theravada school of Buddhism is prevalent, he is also known as Gautama Buddha. It is now generally agreed that Gautama was his family name, the designation given to the particular branch of the Shakya tribe to which he belonged.

Finally, in historical accounts, one often comes across the name *Sid-*

dhartha, which appears to have been the childhood or given name of Shakyamuni. Like the term *Buddha*, this too has a special significance in Sanskrit and may be translated "a goal achieved" or "justice done." According to *Praising the Buddha's Deeds*, Shakyamuni was given this name because upon his birth the kingdom of the Shakyas became rich and prosperous, and all the wishes of his father, Shuddhodana, were fulfilled. Some scholars claim, however, that *Siddhartha* was not actually a name of Shakyamuni but a term of respect applied to him by his followers in later ages in honor of his enlightenment.

THE SHAKYA TRIBE

The tribe into which Shakyamuni was born is said to have had its headquarters in a walled town or city called Kapilavastu. Its exact geographical location has long been a matter of dispute, though it is reported to have been in the southern foothills of the Himalayas, north of the area where the Ganges River spreads out to form a delta. The most recent archaeological studies indicate that it was in the Terai region of the present country of Nepal. According to traditional accounts, however, Shakyamuni was born not in the city itself but in the Lumbini Gardens, which were situated some fifteen miles from Kapilavastu.

By the time of Shakyamuni's birth, a number of cities had grown up in this region of India, and it is probable that Kapilavastu was not very large as cities at that time went, especially in comparison to such major centers as Rajagriha, the capital of the state of Magadha. The Chinese monk and pilgrim Xuanzang (600–664) in *Da Tang xiyu ji* [The Record of the Western Regions of the Great Tang Dynasty], his account of his travels to India, remarks that the climate of the land of the Shakyas was warm and the land quite fertile. The early Buddhist scriptures contain frequent mention of rice, an indication that the people of the time relied mainly upon farming for their subsistence.

We will do best, perhaps, to imagine Kapilavastu as a rather quiet country town.

As to the population of the area, we are told that the Shakya and Koliya tribes together numbered, surprisingly, some one million people. This figure, of course, is no indication of the size of the population of the city of Kapilavastu itself, nor can we suppose that it is based upon any kind of accurate census. In any event, it seems an excessively large number for tribes of rather minor importance, such as the Shakyas and Koliyas, and it is probably safe to assume that, as so often is done in early literature, the figure of a million is intended to mean merely "numerous."

There has been considerable discussion as to what racial stock the Shakyas belonged. The British historian Vincent Smith has put forth the theory that Shakyamuni belonged to a Gurkha-like hill tribe with racial characteristics close to those of the Tibetans, which would make him a member of the Mongol race. This supposition is based upon recent surveys that indicate that the foothills of the Himalayas were at one time inhabited by people of Tibeto-Burman stock.

More common, however, is the view that Shakyamuni and his fellow tribesmen were of Indo-Aryan descent. Support for this view, it is claimed, is found in the fact that the Shakyas spoke proudly of themselves as "descendants of the sun," and that this custom of claiming descent from the sun was widespread among peoples of Indo-Aryan stock. The ancient Vedic hymns of India, in fact, indicate that the god of the sun was among the earliest deities worshiped by the Indo-Aryan peoples. Moreover, texts in Chinese often refer to the Shakyas as the "sun seed people," a further indication that they claimed a special relationship with the sun and hence were Indo-Aryan.

It seems to me rather far-fetched, however, to infer Indo-Aryan ancestry from the fact of sun worship alone, since this is a form of religion common to almost all peoples of ancient times. One has only to think of the worship of the sun goddess Amaterasu in Japan. Moreover, there are numerous instances of ruling families in ancient times that claimed to be actual descendants of the sun. The sun was the most universally recognized object of worship among the peoples of antiquity, and for Shakyamuni to claim that he was a "descendant of the sun" might simply have been a way of paying respect and honor to his ancestors.

A further complication is introduced by the fact that the scriptures speak of Shakyamuni as being descended from a mythical ancestor named Ikshvaku, or Sugar Cane King, the founder of the royal family of the Puru tribe. In the Vedas, the earliest scriptures of the Indo-Aryan settlers of India, the Puru people are described as the enemies of the Indo-Aryans. Some scholars claim, therefore, that if in fact the Sugar Cane King was recognized as the ancestor of Shakyamuni and his people, they could not have been members of the Indo-Aryan race.

Finally, I do not think that it is possible to determine for certain the racial origin of Shakyamuni, who lived so many centuries ago. It cannot be denied, however, that in the ways of thinking associated with Buddhism, there are characteristics that strongly suggest some connection with the Indo-Aryan peoples and their culture. Whatever the racial origin of its founder, there is no doubt that Buddhism grew up within the Indo-Aryan cultural sphere.

THE HISTORICAL SETTING

What can be known about the political situation in India around the time Shakyamuni is said to have lived? The Buddhist scriptures and other writings speak of the sixteen great kingdoms, apparently tribal states that were struggling with one another for domination. Among these, the most prominent were the states of Magadha, Kosala, Vriji, Vatsa, and Avanti. In addition to these larger states, we find mention of various tribes, such as the Baggas, Bulis, Moriyas, Mallas, and the Koliyas and Shakyas already mentioned above.

Of these great kingdoms, that of Kosala, ruled by King Prasenajit, and Magadha, ruled by King Bimbisara, were the most important. The latter in particular, profiting from King Bimbisara's political wisdom and resourcefulness, in time absorbed Kosala and Vriji and founded the imperial dynasty known as the Maurya. The third ruler of that dynasty was the famous emperor Ashoka, who in the third century BCE succeeded in uniting all except the southern tip of the Indian continent under his rule.

During the time when Shakyamuni taught, Magadha was still a newcomer among the contenders for power. Only after King Bimbisara came to the throne did it expand rapidly, extending its power outward from its base along the middle reaches of the Ganges until it controlled much of the region of present-day Bihar, south of the Ganges.

During the so-called period of the sixteen great kingdoms, the Shakyas appear to have been in a relatively weak position. Their base in Kapilavastu was not, as we have seen, a center of great importance or power. In fact, the Shakyas were probably politically dependent upon Kosala, the powerful state to the west that controlled most of the eastern part of what is today Uttar Pradesh. This is indicated by a passage in the early scriptures that describes how Shakyamuni journeyed south along the Ganges and had an interview with King Bimbisara, the ruler of Magadha. In response to questions by the king, Shakyamuni replied that he was a member of a tribe "that from ancient times has been dependent upon Kosala."

We may conclude, then, that the Shakyas were the rulers of a small semiautonomous state that had its capital at Kapilavastu and was dependent upon the kingdom of Kosala to the west. Scholars disagree as to the exact political structure of such small tribal states. Some view them as aristocratic republics ruled by a council of tribal elders who deliberated on policies of state. To support this view, they point out that the ruler of the Shakyas is said to have been elected by a ten-man group of leaders from among their midst. Other scholars, however, see the tribal states of India during this time as moving in the direction of a single powerful and highly centralized state, and surmise that, if they were not actual autocracies, they were at least oligarchies ruled by a select few.

Whatever the internal political structure of the Shakya state may have been, it is certain that it was small and weak and was almost inevitably destined to be annexed by one or another of the great kingdoms that surrounded it on all sides. Shakyamuni was the son of the ruler of this small tribal state whose fortunes were clearly on the decline. On his shoulders would someday fall the task of guiding it through its dark and precarious future, and for this very reason the expectations placed on him were undoubtedly great. What he himself thought of his position and the possibility of fulfilling such expectations had, we may be sure, a very important bearing upon his later decision to renounce the city of Kapilavastu and his role as heir to its throne and embark upon a life of religious austerity.

SHAKYAMUNI'S FAMILY

Before considering the motives that led Shakyamuni to renounce the princely life, let us see if we can form a clearer picture of him as a person by examining what can be known about the immediate members of his family.

His father, as mentioned earlier, was Shuddhodana, a name that in the early Chinese translations of the Buddhist scriptures was rendered as Jing-fan-wang, or Pure Rice King. How, one may ask, did he come to have such a curious name? The Sanskrit actually means "pure milk gruel" and refers to a food made by boiling rice in milk with beans and butter added. This was looked upon as the greatest delicacy of the time, and the name was apparently given to Shakyamuni's father because, as leader of the Shakya tribe, it was appropriate to imagine that he dined upon this finest of foods. The title gives further evidence that the Shakyas were primarily an agricultural and pastoral people. In addition, it is important to note, as pointed out by the noted Buddhist scholar Hajime Nakamura, that Shakyamuni's father was styled merely "king" rather than "great king" as was customary with the rulers of the more powerful states of the time, another indication of the relative weakness of the Shakya tribe.

Shakyamuni's mother is commonly referred to as Queen Maya. The scriptures honor her with the epithet "Great Maya" and employ various complimentary phrases to describe her, but they give very little indication of her identity. Presumably she was the daughter of an influential family of the Shakya tribe, and legend adds that she was related on her mother's side to the Koliya tribe, which evidently lived in close proximity to the Shakyas. The early scriptures preserve an account of a dispute over water rights between the Shakyas and the Koliyas, and some scholars have inferred from this that the two tribes lived on either side of the Rohini River.

According to traditional accounts, Queen Maya gave birth to Shakyamuni in the Lumbini Gardens when she was on her way from Kapilavastu to visit her family and died a week later. The child was brought up by his maternal aunt Mahaprajapati.

It has been speculated that the premature death of his mother, when he learned of it later, may have awakened the young prince to the transitory nature of life and led him to renounce his royal home. Whether the knowledge of his mother's death was what actually impelled him to turn to the religious life seems to me questionable. But to a young man of great emotional sensitivity, as I imagine the youthful Shakyamuni to have been, the death of any close relative was bound to have come as a profound shock and to have impressed upon him that suffering is an inevitable part of all human life.

~

SHAKYAMUNI'S EARLY YEARS

The sensitive nature of the young Shakyamuni is further indicated by a passage in the scriptures in which, after entering the religious life and attaining enlightenment, he looks back on his early years and says: "Although brought up in wealth, I was by nature very sensitive, and it caused me to wonder why, when all men are destined to suffer old age, sickness, and death, and none can escape these things, they yet look upon the old age, sickness, and death of other men with fear, loathing, and scorn. This is not right, I thought, and at that time all the joy of youth and the pride and courage I felt in my own good health deserted me."

Regarding his physical appearance, he was described in later times as being endowed with "thirty-two distinguishing features and eighty physical characteristics." The thirty-two distinguishing features include very long fingers, arms that reach to the knees, forty teeth, and other abnormal characteristics that, if he actually possessed them, would have made him some kind of monster. However, I do not think we need to take such descriptions literally. Brahmanism, the dominant religion in India in Shakyamuni's time, contains a similar concept of thirty-two unusual features that distinguish the *chakravartin*, or "wheel-turning king," the ideal ruler. It is probable that the disciples of Shakyamuni, in their desire to exalt their great master and indicate what a perfect person he was, simply borrowed the thirty-two distinguishing physical features from Brahmanism and applied them to the Buddha.

Continuing the passage of reminiscence quoted above, Shakyamuni says of himself that he was "slender in build, very delicate, and was brought up with great care." Although he may have been rather thin and high strung, we need not necessarily imagine him as a pale, bookish type of boy. He was, after all, a king's son and had to undergo the kind of training that would enable him to take over the throne from his father when the time came.

Legend, in fact, asserts that Shuddhodana saw to it that his son, upon whose shoulders would rest the fate of the Shakya clan, was given instruction in both the civil and the military arts. Because Shakyamuni was by nature rather an introspective and philosophical youth, his father no doubt took special care to provide him with proper physical as well as intellectual and moral education. This is perhaps what Shakyamuni meant when he said that he was "brought up with great care."

In addition, Shakyamuni states that his underwear and other garments were all made of silk and that a parasol was held over his head all day long. He had three palaces, one for winter, one for summer, and one for the rainy season, where he lived surrounded by ladies-in-waiting, dancers, and musicians to serve and entertain him. Whether or not every detail of this description is to be taken literally, it gives some indication of the care and lavish attention with which the young prince was brought up.

Another episode recorded in the scriptures gives some indication of Shakyamuni's physical appearance. After entering the religious life, he is said to have visited the state of Magadha and had an interview with King Bimbisara. The latter was so impressed with Shakyamuni's upright bearing and appearance that he begged him to become the leader of the army of Magadha. Needless to say, Shakyamuni refused this request. We do not know how much training he had had in the military arts, but it is clear that, to have inspired the king to make such a request, there must have been something in his appearance and bearing that marked him as a natural leader of men.

In his youth it was no doubt the fate of his own people that weighed most heavily on his mind, as he was well aware that the Shakya state was small and weak and constantly threatened by its neighbors. His keen sensibility and devotion to justice must have kept him pondering day and night some way to lead his people to safety. He was given to meditation and introspection in spite of the warm and inviting surroundings in which he was raised, and this was because he was deeply concerned about the future role of leader that he was destined to play. The youthful Shakyamuni, I believe, can best be described as a humanist and seeker after truth who had a keen sense of justice.

Among the most important events of Shakyamuni's youthful years was his marriage to Yashodhara. Some legends say that he won her in a test of arms with various rivals, including his cousin Devadatta. It is even asserted that, after Shakyamuni had attained enlightenment and gone abroad on a preaching tour to other parts of India, Devadatta went to Kapilavastu and attempted to seduce Yashodhara in her husband's absence. Although Shakyamuni and Devadatta were cousins, however, they were apparently quite far apart in age, and there is probably no truth to the story that they were rivals for the hand of Yashodhara.

Yashodhara herself was a cousin of Shakyamuni, though beyond this fact almost nothing is recorded concerning her. No doubt this is due in part to the fact that Shakyamuni's disciples and followers in later years were interested primarily in his life after he had renounced his family and attained enlightenment and therefore paid scant attention to the events of his youthful years. It may also be an indication that Yashodhara did not play a very decisive role in her husband's life but was, rather, modest and reserved, as befitted an Indian woman of noble birth. Had she been noted for a bad temper, like Socrates' wife, history would perhaps have preserved a fuller account of her. But the wives of great philosophers and thinkers do not, generally speaking, appear in the limelight, and Yashodhara is no exception.

It is not certain at what age Shakyamuni married; some accounts say that he was sixteen, others that he was nineteen or older. Yashodhara bore him one child, a son named Rahula, who later became one of the Buddha's ten principal disciples. On this point all accounts are in agreement, but beyond this nothing is known of Shakyamuni's married life. If one accepts the theory that he married at sixteen, it is easy to imagine that his father, concerned about the future of his introspective son, arranged an early marriage for him in hopes that he would quickly settle down and prepare himself for the succession to the throne.

For Shakyamuni himself, the wedding, no matter how glittering and sumptuous, could not dispel from his mind the deep anxiety that he felt over the questions of old age, sickness, and death, nor could the joys of married life. Meanwhile, Rahula was born. This was an event of great importance, for it meant that Shakyamuni now had an heir to carry on the line of succession, and he himself was free, if he wished, to renounce his claim to the throne and enter the religious life.

THE GREAT
DEPARTURE 2

There are various theories as to how old Shakyamuni was when he determined to leave his home and family and enter upon the religious life, an event that was to change not only his life but the entire spiritual history of the world. Some sources record that he was nineteen when he took this momentous step, others that he was twenty-nine. If we accept the former, this would mean that, having married around the age of sixteen and fathered a son, he very soon made up his mind to renounce family life and seek enlightenment. As we shall describe in detail further on, he thereafter studied under two Brahman sages but, dissatisfied with their instruction, left to practice religious austerities on his own.

After pursuing austerities until he had reduced himself to emaciation, he became aware that such practices would not lead to emancipation. Finally he seated himself at the foot of a pipal tree in the forest near Buddhagaya, fell into deep meditation, and there achieved enlightenment. According to most accounts, he was thirty at the time. If we regard him as having renounced his family at the age of nineteen, that would mean that he spent a period of twelve years in his quest for the true Way. The earliest scriptures, however, represent Shakyamuni as having said in his own words that he entered upon the religious life at the age of twenty-nine and that he achieved enlightenment seven years later—that is, when he was thirty-five or thirty-six years of age.

We touched earlier upon the political situation in northern India at the time and mentioned that the Shakya state was constantly threatened by more powerful neighbors, particularly the state of Magadha. If one of the considerations that led Shakyamuni to renounce the worldly life was his despair over the waning political fortunes of his own tribe, then it is more likely that he did so around the age of thirty. Magadha was a relative newcomer to the struggle for political supremacy and only reached important status after King Bimbisara came to the throne. King Bimbisara became ruler of Magadha at age fifteen, and we are told that he was five years younger than Shakyamuni. Shakyamuni would already have been in his twenties, therefore, when he witnessed the rapid expansion in the power and fortunes of the state of Magadha and came to realize what a threat they posed to the survival of his own people.

In the end, however, we can only guess how old Shakyamuni may have been when he entered upon the religious life. More important, I believe, is to probe more deeply into the motives that impelled him to take such a step, since these are intimately related to the nature of the enlightenment that he achieved and indeed to the very essence of Buddhism as a religion.

Tradition offers the so-called four meetings as the reason for Shakyamuni's departure for the religious life. According to early accounts, Shakyamuni was for the most part confined to the royal palace and was shielded by his father from exposure to any knowledge of worldly woes. On four occasions, however, he succeeded in venturing beyond the palace gates in the company of his charioteer. Emerging from the eastern gate of the palace on what was intended to be a pleasure excursion, Shakyamuni was confronted by the sight of an old man; emerging from the south gate on another occasion, he saw a sick man; and when he left by the west gate, he saw a corpse. Finally, going out the north gate, he spied a man who had entered the religious life, and, deeply moved, he determined to leave home and take up the same kind of life himself.

Such an anecdote, with its neat symmetry, differs in nature, of course, from what we would call an objective historical account of events. Yet it serves to sum up in symbolic form the process by which Shakyamuni was led to renounce the world in that it focuses attention upon what is the essential starting point of the Buddhist religion—the question of human suffering.

Shakyamuni, a sensitive and philosophical youth, undoubtedly pondered the essence of life and attempted, through his keen and probing intellect, to discover answers to the questions that filled his mind concerning it. We can justly infer from his later teachings that he was particularly vexed by the problems of birth, old age, sickness, and death—sufferings that were inevitably bound up with the very existence of man. The force that impelled him to take up the religious life, and indeed became the point of departure for the entire Buddhist religion, was an ardent desire to transcend the sufferings inherent in human life.

What are human beings? What is life? These were the questions that Shakyamuni put to himself. And since humanity and human life are in the end only one part of the mysterious life force that, moment by moment, pulses through the world, he went on to inquire about the nature of that life force itself. It is because Buddhism addresses itself to such fundamental questions of life and existence that it has continued to flourish, its light undimmed by the centuries.

Apart from his wish to find a solution to the problem of human suffering, it has been suggested that, in his decision to enter the religious life, Shakyamuni was also strongly influenced by his introspective temperament and by the inauspicious social and political situation faced by the people of the Shakya tribe. Although there is no doubt that he agonized over the fate that seemed to lie in store for his people, this does not mean that the only course left open to him was to become a religious ascetic. Since he was the heir apparent to the throne, one logical solution would have been for him to consider raising an army and challenging the power of his neighbors. But this course he did not choose to take. I would like to think that he instinctively rejected it because of his deeply humanitarian nature.

In general, the young men of India in Shakyamuni's time, particularly those belonging to noble or powerful families, dreamed of two ideals. One was to become a *chakravartin*, or "wheel-turning king," a great leader who would guide his kingdom to a position of supremacy in the temporal world. The other was to become a Buddha, an enlightened sage who would act as a spiritual teacher to the men and women of his age. Shakyamuni, it seems, quite consciously chose to pursue the latter ideal.

Though he lived in the luxury of the royal palace, what Shakyamuni saw when he turned his eyes beyond the palace were the daily struggles and sufferings of the ordinary men and women of the Shakya tribe. Those about him did their best to hide such unpleasant sights from him, but the more they tried to shield him from reality, the deeper and keener did this sensitive young man become in his determination to confront it. The legend of the four excursions outside the palace gates conveys in symbolic form the workings of his mind at this time.

Because Shakyamuni knew that military force can never bring about a lasting solution to the problem of human suffering, he did not attempt to assist his people by any resort to arms but instead embarked on the road that he hoped in time would lead to sagehood. Rather than become a king who wields political power in the temporal world, he chose to become a philosopher-king in the metaphysical realm. Rather than seek some fleeting moment of glory for his people in the ever-changing world of political power, he chose to bestow upon them a joy that is everlasting and changeless, founded upon essential truth.

Shakyamuni clearly renounced all claim to kingship in the temporal world. His disciples in later ages nevertheless often bestowed upon him the title of *chakravartin*, or ideal monarch. The fact that such a title, originally appropriate only for a political or social leader, should have been applied to a leader in the spiritual realm has sometimes been interpreted as an indication that Shakyamuni and his disciples suffered from a kind of political inferiority complex, which they sought to counter with an impression of worldly success. This assertion, however, seems extremely doubtful. It was common for early Buddhists to take concepts and terms prevalent in Brahmanism and adapt them to their own use. In adopting the term *chakravartin* and applying it to the Buddha, their purpose, I believe, was simply to emphasize the universal validity of Shakyamuni's teachings.

With regard to Shakyamuni's decision to leave his home and take up the religious life, it should be borne in mind that in ancient India, such a step never implied an attitude of pessimism or despair. Nowadays, those who take up the religious life are often thought of as leaving ordinary life and entering a world apart. But this was not true in ancient India, which had a long and well-established tradition of asceticism and spiritual quest. In Shakyamuni's time it was not uncommon for men of intellectual bent to leave their homes, enter the forest, and seek to discover the truth of human existence. Far from being looked upon as eccentric, such a course of action was not considered unusual.

The only difference in Shakyamuni's case was that he entered upon this phase of his life rather early. This, I believe, was because his passion to discover the truth was far stronger than that of other men. He was not merely complying with the custom of the time but obeying forces that sprang from the inner recesses of his being.

The ascetic life was regarded as a means by which one might pursue philosophical concerns and seek to discover the fundamental truths of human existence. In entering upon such a life, a person naturally removed himself from the ordinary framework of society and culture and, in a sense, repudiated its values. But he did so for purposes of reflection, so that he might discover new ideals and values. Returning once more to the conventional framework of society, he could teach and lead others from the standpoint of a new and higher dimension.

This is why Buddhism, the religion founded by Shakyamuni, has rarely found itself alienated or removed from the society and age in which it exists. It has always been conscious of the need to discover, through some unique philosophical approach, a fundamental solution to the problems of the society and the times in which it functions.

THE ASCETIC AND INDIAN SOCIETY

Just when and under what circumstances did this practice of abandoning one's family and turning to the life of the religious ascetic begin in India? The great poet and philosopher Rabindranath Tagore has observed, "Greek civilization was built out of bricks made of clay, but Indian civilization was born in the forest." I wonder if asceticism in India did not have its genesis in the Indian fascination with the forest and the habit of retiring there to meditate and perfect one's wisdom and understanding. This custom has long been a part of the Indian tradition, and even today there are dense forests in the Ganges River basin where groups of people who have gone into retirement lead a kind of communal life devoted to the search for greater philosophical understanding. It is quite conceivable that, as Tagore has said, Indian civilization and philosophy were born in the forest rather than the city.

There is in early Indian history a period known as the age of the Aranyakas, or "forest treatises." This occurred slightly before the so-called Upanishad period, or some three hundred years before the time of Shakyamuni. It would appear that, as the writings that give their name to the period indicate, the custom of retiring to the forest for meditation dates back at least to this time, which would correspond to the eighth or ninth century BCE.

By Shakyamuni's time, it had become a convention among members of the upper class to retire to the forest for such a period of meditation and reflection. Members of the upper class, which consisted mainly of people belonging to the Brahman class, appear to have divided their life into four distinct periods: (1) *brahmacharin,* or studenthood; (2) *grihastha,* family life; (3) *vanaprastha,* life in the forest; and (4) *sannyasin,* seclusion and wandering.

The first period, that of studenthood, began at age seven or eight and lasted about twelve years, during which time one received instruction from teachers in the doctrines and practices of Brahmanism. Upon completion of these studies, one returned to his family, married, and entered the second phase. This phase, the longest of the four, lasted some thirty years, roughly from the age of twenty to fifty. During this phase of life, a man performed sacrifices to his ancestors and carried out other ritual duties, raised a family of his own, and took an active part in society as the head of a family. When he had fulfilled his duties as head of a family and produced an heir to carry on in his place, he was then free to take up residence in the forest and, while reflecting quietly upon the previous fifty years of his life, could seek to share the life of the natural world about him and attain full philosophical maturity. After this period of asceticism and religious practice was completed, he emerged from the forest and spent the last period of life wandering from place to place in a penniless state, depending upon alms for a livelihood.

This, as will be seen, is a very religiously and philosophically oriented course of life. In the modern world, we could perhaps say that the first phase is equivalent to the period of formal education, the second phase to the years that one devotes to his business or profession before retirement. But there is no equivalent to the third and fourth periods of reflection and wandering.

Of course, the ancient Brahmans lived in a society that was far less complex than that of today, and there were undoubtedly fewer demands upon their time. Moreover, since they represented the highest class in society and had slaves laboring under them to provide the economic necessities of life, they were free to devote themselves to other concerns. But whatever social conditions may have been necessary to make such a convention possible, the fact that the early Brahmans laid out such a four-phased course of life indicates how deeply rooted was the custom of philosophical meditation in Indian life and what great importance the Indians attached to philosophy and religion. It is highly admirable in any people of any age to find them utilizing the few years given to them in this life to examine the realities of human existence and to attempt on the basis of what they discover to formulate some clear personal philosophy. In ancient China as well, we see the desire to correlate the periods of life with some deepening comprehension of the meaning and proper approach to human existence. "At thirty I stood on my own," writes Confucius, "at forty I was free from doubt, at fifty I understood the will of Heaven." In contrast to people of ancient times who appear to have had this sense of advancement and purposeful seeking in their lives, modern human beings seem merely to be buffeted by endless dizzying waves of change and swamped by a vast deluge of knowledge and information that they are powerless to understand or control.

But to return from such melancholy digressions to the subject of ancient India, I do not think we can say with any exactitude just when this four-phased concept of life arose in the Brahman class. It seems to have been in existence long before Shakyamuni's time, however, and therefore provides a useful reference point for understanding his life. When we consider Shakyamuni's life in terms of the four traditional phases, we see at once that he abandoned his family and entered upon the ascetic life during the second rather than the third phase, and quite early in the second phase at that.

It has often been asserted that Shakyamuni was merely following the custom of his class and time when he left home. Far from following custom, however, as we have seen, he left home at a far earlier age than was prescribed by convention, an indication of how intense was his desire to set out in search of the truth. Shakyamuni's entry upon the religious life was motivated by much deeper impulses than those that governed the ordinary follower of convention during his time.

~

THE DEPARTURE AND WANDERINGS

The scriptures contain various legends of a dramatic nature concerning Shakyamuni's actual departure from the palace. Setting aside for the moment those of a patently fictional nature, we may note that Shakyamuni, after arriving at his momentous decision, is said to have confided in his father. This was to be expected, since his father had been worried over Shakyamuni's sensitivity and his strong tendency toward introspection. Shuddhodana had taken special pains to correct these aspects of Shakyamuni's character over the course of his upbringing. If we accept the account of the scriptures, Shuddhodana would already have had forebodings of the kind of life that lay in store for his son, for after Shakyamuni was born at the Lumbini Gardens and brought to the palace in Kapilavastu, his father sent for a renowned soothsayer named Asita and asked him to prophesy Shakyamuni's future. After examining the features of the newborn child, Asita concluded: "He has signs that indicate that he may become a universal monarch who will rule the world or that he may become a Buddha who will renounce family life and lead the world to salvation. But though he has signs indicating either possibility, I believe that this prince will surely become a Buddha!"

One is tempted to dismiss this legend as merely another manifestation of the process of deification that took place after Shakyamuni's enlightenment. On the other hand, soothsaying, astrology, and other methods of divination were common practices in the society of

Shakyamuni's time, and there is nothing surprising in Shuddhodana's calling in a diviner to foretell his son's future. As to the actual content of Asita's prophecy, I believe we can interpret it as a tribute to some indefinable quality about the infant Shakyamuni that set him apart from ordinary men.

We find such prophecies recorded about many famous historical personages. They had about them, even in infancy, we are told, a nobility of expression, an intrepid demeanor, or a winning gentleness that presaged some extraordinary future. Shakyamuni, too, is described in the scriptures as having lustrous features that held the gaze of the people around him "like the moon" and limbs that "shone with the radiance of precious gold." Such descriptions may be no more than the inventions of zealous disciples of later years. Still, it is not surprising that the seer Asita found something arresting and unusual in the features of the infant Shakyamuni and that his predictions of future Buddhahood helped to foster Shuddhodana's apprehension concerning his moody son.

Shakyamuni was undoubtedly fully aware of his father's fears, and therefore when he finally arrived at his decision to renounce family life, he forthrightly reported his intentions to his father. Though the news could not have come as a total surprise, Shuddhodana was shocked by the gravity of his son's decision, and he attempted to dissuade him.

As a last resort, Shuddhodana is said to have taken forcible measures to prevent his son's departure from the city. Finally, however, mounted on his beloved steed Kanthaka and accompanied by his attendant Chandaka, Shakyamuni made his way out of the city of Kapilavastu.

Shakyamuni first entered the territory of the Koliyas and from there journeyed south across the Anouma River. Then he cut off his hair, removed all his jewelry and ornaments, handed them over to Chandaka, and sent the latter back to Kapilavastu with the message that he would not return to the city until he had fulfilled the objective for which he had entered the religious life and attained enlightenment.

From that point on, he journeyed alone, dressed as a religious mendicant, making his way south through the states of Mana and Vriji in the direction of Magadha.

The distance from Kapilavastu to Rajagriha, the capital of Magadha, was about 373 miles. Since there seems to have been considerable commercial activity in those times, it is probable that he followed a trade route running through the area. We know that, in later years, after his enlightenment, he often traveled with trade caravans when he embarked on his proselytizing journeys.

But before describing Shakyamuni's activities in Magadha, let us return to two points touched on above. The first is the fact that Shakyamuni cut off his hair when he entered the religious life. Some scholars maintain that the custom of tonsuring was already practiced by some Brahman ascetics before Shakyamuni's time. After his time, however, it came to be regarded as a special mark of members of the Buddhist Order, and records tell us that members of that Order were referred to as *munda*, a word meaning "tonsured one." Ascetics of other religious groups in the period before Shakyamuni, if they practiced tonsuring at all, must not have done so in anything like the consistent fashion of the Buddhists. Brahmans, as we know from epithets applied to them, were conspicuous for wearing their hair tied up or braided, while the followers of Jainism, as part of their ascetic practices, pulled out the hairs from their head and beard one by one. Although the practice of tonsuring may have existed before Shakyamuni, after Shakyamuni and his disciples it came to be associated particularly with the followers of Buddhism.

The second point worth noting is that Shakyamuni adopted the garb of a religious mendicant. In Shakyamuni's time, the custom of mendicancy, or begging for alms, was widely practiced by those who had entered upon the homeless life and was therefore looked upon as a conventional and perhaps even a commendable form of behavior. The practice probably dates back a number of centuries before

Shakyamuni's time and may be as old as the pursuit of the ascetic life itself.

A person who has embarked upon the ascetic life and completed his religious training was called a *bhikkhu* (Skt *bhikshu*), a Pali word meaning "one who begs for food." In ancient India, such people were looked upon with great respect, and ordinary people were only too happy to feed them. This was because it was believed that by doing so one could acquire a store of good karma, or causes leading to good effects for oneself. Far from being obsequious or fawning in their requests, such mendicants are said to have walked the streets with an air of great dignity, clad in proper robes rather than the rags of ordinary beggars. When they had received an offering, they quickly took their departure without bothering to thank the almsgiver who, after all, had increased their store of merit. If the mendicants' presence at the door were unnoticed by the members of the family, they would shake the metal rings attached to the tips of their staves to attract attention. Such behavior would seem to indicate that the practice of almsgiving itself was steeped in religious significance.

On the other hand, the person receiving alms, if it was a gift of food, was expected to eat it with a sense of gratitude, no matter how simple or even unsavory it might be. In this respect, I wonder if mendicancy, and the attendant obligation to eat whatever food was offered to one, did not in some sense represent a form of challenge or protest against the taboos of Indian society.

The taboos I refer to were the rigid rules governing the class and caste system of ancient India, under which all people were divided into four major classes: the Brahman, or priestly class; the Kshatriya, or warrior class; the Vaishyas, who were merchants and landowners; and the Shudras, peasants or serfs belonging to the aboriginal population. In addition to these basic class divisions, various caste divisions grew up in time. Members of different castes were forbidden to intermarry, eat together, or associate freely, and one could not even eat food that had been prepared by a person of another caste. Such restrictions were observed with particular punctiliousness by the members of the higher castes, who would rather starve to death than eat food that came from the hands of a person of inferior caste and hence was ritually defiled. In this rigidly segregated society of ancient India, the figure of the religious mendicant, wandering about from village to village and eating whatever was given to him, certainly presents an anomaly.

As mentioned above, a *bhikkhu* was originally a person who had completed his period of training in the ascetic life and was respected by the population at large for that reason. This concept changed over the centuries, however, until just before Shakyamuni's time, when ascetics appeared who looked upon mendicancy itself as a form of religious practice. This new group of mendicant ascetics included thinkers who refused to recognize the restrictions of the traditional Brahman social system and who sought deliberately to challenge and break away from the old order. They were able to do this all the more effectively because of the great respect traditionally accorded in India to one who had embarked upon the ascetic life.

As mentioned already, the two types of ideal people in ancient Indian thought were the universal monarch and the enlightened sage. The mendicant represented the latter, the person who had already completed the practices leading to enlightenment or at least was far advanced in that direction. Finding oneself in the presence of an embodiment of this ideal, it was only natural to be filled with anticipation and awe and, while gladly presenting offerings of food, to hope that one's own karmic destiny might benefit from the meeting. Respect for the man of religion runs very deep in Indian society, where the highest of the four classes was that of the Brahmans, or priests. Therefore it came to be felt that when one met with a true man of religion, class and caste distinctions could be forgotten in the act of presenting him with one's wholehearted offering.

~

THE RISE OF A NEW CULTURE

Shakyamuni traveled south, as we have said, with the state of Magadha as his final destination. Various suggestions have been put forward as to why he chose Magadha rather than one of the other states of the time. The most powerful of these were Magadha and Kosala. But the latter, as we have seen, was situated close to Shakyamuni's native state and dominated it politically. If he had gone to Kosala and it had been discovered there that he, the prince of a dependent state, had entered the religious life, there would undoubtedly have been considerable comment. It is even possible that he would have been forcibly sent back to Kapilavastu, the city from which he had only recently managed with great effort to escape. It was probably with this thought in mind that he chose to journey to Magadha, where the danger of enforced repatriation was much less.

Aside from such personal reasons, it is probable that Shakyamuni chose to go to Magadha because he saw it as the center of a new culture that was just then coming into being. Indian society was at this time undergoing a process of radical change. The members of the Brahman class, who had previously been looked upon almost as divine beings, were beginning to lose their authority, and the traditional patterns of the society over which they had presided were likewise changing.

Partly this change was the result of corruption and degeneracy within the ranks of the Brahmans themselves, but it was hastened by sweeping social changes that took place as the Aryan invaders, who had entered India from the northwest some centuries earlier, continued to expand their power to the east and south. With the growth of commerce and trade, rich merchants of the Vaishya class appeared who, because of their wealth and power, could challenge the authority of the Brahmans. In addition, as the territorial expansion of the Aryans progressed, members of the Kshatriya class, who fought the battles and acted as political leaders of the newly formed states, likewise rose in authority until their power was greater than that of their nominal superiors, the priestly Brahmans.

Shortly before and during the time of Shakyamuni, we find the members of the Kshatriya class challenging the Brahmans not only in matters of social power and precedence but in the fields of philosophy and religion as well. The Upanishads, religious writings that date from a period slightly later than that of the Aranyakas, or forest treatises, give evidence of the challenge posed by the Kshatriyas to the authority of the Brahmans. In one, we are told of a king who openly argued with a Brahman and pointed out fallacies in the Brahman religious doctrines. According to the account, the Brahman sage admitted defeat and in turn begged the king to become his teacher. Such anecdotes give evidence that the Kshatriyas were beginning to surpass the Brahmans in both social and intellectual position. In addition, the entire philosophy underlying the Upanishads, with its skepticism and ceaseless questioning of accepted beliefs, may be said to represent the outlook of this group newly rising to power in society.

These new leaders of the Kshatriya class, along with the new class of wealthy merchants known as *shreshthin,* departed from the patterns of the old tribal society of the Brahmans and worked to build a new kind of social structure headed by a monarch. In Shakyamuni's time, these social changes were taking place with great rapidity, and at the center of the new society and culture that were beginning to emerge was the state of Magadha.

History shows that the truly great and epoch-making philosophers, thinkers, and revolutionaries of the world first acquaint themselves with the finest culture and ideology of their time before going on to transcend them and establish their own original system of philosophy. Shakyamuni no doubt chose to go to Magadha because he wished to confront the new culture and thought that were evolving there. It is important to note that it was in Magadha also that he practiced religious austerities, attained enlightenment, and first preached the Buddhist religion, and that among his early converts were King Bimbisara of Magadha and many of the *shreshthin,* or wealthy merchants, of that state. In addition, King Prasenajit of Kosala also respected Shakyamuni and supported his religious activities. Buddhism, it would seem, was able fully to reflect and absorb the tendencies and modes of thought of the new culture and society and in time became the religion most commonly associated with it.

This does not mean, of course, that Buddhism addressed itself only to merchants and members of the ruling class. It was from the beginning a religion that repudiated all class and caste distinctions and appealed to all people alike, regardless of their position in society. Nevertheless, the assistance given by wealthy merchants to the Buddhist Order is often mentioned in the scriptures. One of them donated the Bamboo Grove Monastery in Rajagriha, and another a monastery in the city of Shravasti in Kosala. The best known of these patrons was Sudatta, said to have been the richest man in Kosala, who also became known by the name Anathapindada, or "Supplier of the Needy," because of the generous way in which he shared his wealth with the poor.

One of the most important and distinctive features of this new culture that was growing up in Magadha and Kosala was the appearance of thinkers who openly repudiated the Vedic tradition and the authority of the old Brahman social order. Their appearance is very important, for it indicates just how radical were the changes taking place in society, with men daring to free themselves entirely from the doctrines of Brahmanism.

These men were known by the term *shramana,* which means "one who practices religious austerities." Originally this term was applied to all ascetics in general—that is, to men who, in the four traditional phases of life described earlier, had embarked upon the third phase and entered the forest to practice austerities and meditation. By Shakyamuni's time, the word had come to mean those ascetics who refused to accept Brahmanism and the social order that it represented.

Magadha seems to have been a gathering place for these *shramanas*. Shakyamuni later came to be called Gautama Shramana, because he was regarded as belonging to this group of reformist thinkers. Although at the outset he undoubtedly explored the new schools of thought that were springing up, the enlightenment that he eventually attained was of a wholly different order from anything dreamed of by the other *shramanas* of the time.

THE SIX NON-BUDDHIST TEACHERS

To define the doctrines taught by these new thinkers of Shakyamuni's time is no easy task, since they were far from agreeing with one another and propounded a great variety of ideas. The Buddhist scriptures, however, mention six men who were leaders among the thinkers of the *shramana* group. Known as the six heretical or non-Buddhist teachers, they are Makkhali Gosala, Purana Kassapa, Ajita Kesakambala, Pakudha Kacchayana, Sanjaya Belatthiputta, and Nigantha Nataputta.

Of these, the most famous is Nigantha Nataputta, who founded the religion known as Jainism. He was a member of the Kshatriya class and a son of the noble and prestigious Licchavi tribe, but he left his family and took up the ascetic life, seeking liberation through rigorous discipline and a strict suppression of all desire. One of the most important prohibitions placed upon the followers of the Jain religion is that against the taking of life. This injunction is interpreted with extreme rigor, so that one must take elaborate precautions to prevent the inadvertent killing of even a tiny insect.

While the injunction against the taking of life and other precepts of the Jains bear a considerable resemblance to the five precepts set forth by Shakyamuni, in spirit Buddhism rejects the extreme asceticism enjoined by Nigantha Nataputta upon his followers. For a time, Shakyamuni himself practiced such extreme austerities but abandoned them when he realized that they merely inflicted suffering upon the body and did not lead to enlightenment.

Another thinker, one who seems to have enjoyed a considerable following among the intellectuals of the time, was Ajita Kesakambala. Declaring that everything in the universe was made up of the four basic elements of earth, water, fire, and wind, he taught a doctrine of thoroughgoing materialism. Since the world was comprised of matter alone, nothing remained of life when the body died, and it was therefore of no consequence whether he performed good or evil deeds in his lifetime.

The popularity of such an amoralistic doctrine reflects the intellectual climate of the age. The religious teachings of Brahmanism, which previously had been looked upon as sacred and inviolable, had been challenged and in some cases openly rejected. This naturally led to a questioning of the moral precepts taught by Brahmanism as well. This negativistic attitude toward traditional moral standards was a trait shared by all six non-Buddhist thinkers. In one sense, this type of thinking represented a great step forward, since it implied an attempt to free man from his fear of the wrath of the gods and from the merciless restrictions of a hierarchical social system. On the other hand, one cannot deny that such philosophies had a tendency to degenerate into nihilism and moral decadence. In this respect, Shakyamuni, though he was called *shramana,* differed greatly from these thinkers, since there was nothing of this antisocial element in his teachings.

Sanjaya Belatthiputta, another of the six non-Buddhist teachers, was noted for his nihilism and skepticism. He questioned the doctrine of the immortality of the atman, or Self, as expounded in the Upanishads, and denied the eternal principle of Brahman, maintaining that no such eternal and unchanging principle exists.

Among Sanjaya Belatthiputta's most outstanding disciples were two men named Shariputra and Maudgalyayana who, growing dissatisfied with the nihilism and negativism of their teacher's doctrines, decided to become followers of Buddhism, being deeply impressed by the pure and holy aspect of one of Shakyamuni's disciples whom they chanced to meet. When they left Sanjaya, some 250 other followers are reported to have joined them. In time, Shariputra and Maudgalyayana came to be numbered among the ten great disciples of the Buddha. According to legend, Sanjaya was so distressed at losing two of his most promising disciples that he spat up blood. If he was a true skeptic, however, the incident must have convinced him more than ever of the rightness of his views.

The same questioning of traditional moral values is found in the teachings of Makkhali Gosala, who expounded an extreme form of fatalism. Since everything in the world, according to him, appeared and perished in accordance with the ineluctable laws of karma, or causality, no amount of devotional effort or practice of religious austerities could have any effect upon the strictly fated course of events. He therefore counseled acceptance of the doctrine of *samsara,* or transmigration, as expounded in the Upanishads, and indeed maintained that there was no alternative. His was a prototype of the philosophy of total resignation that is popularly referred to by the phrase *que será será,* "what will be will be."

In direct contradiction of Makkhali Gosala's views, Purana Kassapa denied the existence of any law of karma and put forward the view that all phenomena were totally without significance. In the end, this nihilistic view led him to deny the social nature of humankind and to reject all concepts of morality and of humankind's proper role in society.

Among these generally nihilistic doctrines, the teachings of Pakudha Kacchayana stand out as something of an exception. To the four material elements of earth, water, fire, and wind expounded by Ajita Kesakambala, he added such spiritual elements as suffering, pleasure, and the soul. He also expounded the doctrine of the immortality and changeless nature of the soul. In his view of life, humankind's foremost duty was to ensure the peace and stability of his soul.

These new thinkers all carried out religious practices based on their various philosophies, and since their doctrines were often extremist in nature and represented a deliberate repudiation of tradition and past history, these practices were similarly drastic and unconventional—including, we are told, sitting naked in the burning heat of the sun, daubing the body all over with mud, eating only the wild grasses that grew in the forest, and in general endeavoring to live the most primitive life.

In terms of ideological atmosphere, their age was in some ways quite like our own. In modern parlance, they were "dropouts" from traditional Brahman society who banded together to live a communal life based on patterns and values of their own. While their behavior often flouted the accepted conventions and common sense, underlying that behavior was the legitimate desire for some new and more satisfying philosophy of life. In all these respects, they resemble the spiritual seekers of our time, who often seem drawn to yoga, Zen, and other facets of Indian and Eastern philosophy. The fact that the doctrines of the six thinkers—even with their strongly materialistic and amoral tendencies and their nihilistic cast—enjoyed considerable popularity is another point that calls for comparison of that period with modern times.

The six thinkers lived at a time when a new class was coming to the fore, and profound changes were taking place in Indian society. In this period of rapidly shifting values, the six teachers acted as standard-bearers for the new forces that were seeking to demolish the rigid system of values created earlier by Brahmanism. The markedly nihilistic and negativistic tendencies in their thought were probably no more than reflections of the general philosophical temper of the times. But with a negativistic philosophy alone one cannot foster the kind of spirit that will create a new society. This was the limitation inherent in their thought. Among the religious philosophies of the day, it was only Buddhism, the philosophy of Shakyamuni, that transcended negativism and provided a final dialectical resolution of the problems raised by the conflict between traditional Brahmanism and the forces seeking to overthrow it.

But we should not regard the appearance of the six teachers and the philosophy of Shakyamuni simply as events that took place long ago in India. For modern people living in a society strongly colored by currents of epicureanism, nihilism, and decadence, these events have an important historical message.

The German philosopher Karl Jaspers has pointed out that Shakyamuni was born at almost the same time that Socrates appeared in Greece, Confucius in China, and the prophet Deutero-Isaiah, whose thought exerted such an important influence upon Christianity, in the Judaic world. The collective appearance of these great men within a single era, in Jaspers' view, marks this as the dawn of the spiritual civilization of humankind. In terms of the human spirit, it may be called the first great pivotal era, when the various philosophies propounded by these men made their appearance in response to dramatic changes in ancient society.

Until the nineteenth century, human history continued to unfold on the basis of the spiritual principles evolved at the time of this first pivotal era. But with the twentieth century, the material civilization that humanity had created for itself suddenly began to change, advancing with a wholly unexpected rapidity. What is needed at this point in human history, in Jaspers' opinion, is a new philosophy, a new religion that can cope with the phenomenal growth of science and technology, therefore effectively introducing a second pivotal age.

Thus, when we turn our attention to the life and times of Shakyamuni, it is not simply because we wish to know more about the events of the distant past but because we are concerned for the needs of the present. For when we delve deeply and with true earnestness into the past, who knows what fresh springs of spiritual nourishment may be brought to light? The great interest in Buddhism evident among intellectuals today is fostered, I believe, by hopes of such a discovery.

The noted Buddhist scholar Fumio Masutani has suggested that the relationship between the six non-Buddhist teachers and Shakyamuni resembled that which existed between the Sophists and Socrates. Socrates' teachings in some ways paralleled or drew upon the teachings of the various Sophist philosophers, but at the same time Socrates far surpassed the Sophists dialectically. In the same way, the teachings of Shakyamuni paralleled but far transcended those of the six non-Buddhist teachers. Just as Greek political and cultural life in Socrates' time centered on the city-states of Athens, Sparta, and others, so the life of northern India in Shakyamuni's time was dominated by the city-states of Rajagriha in Magadha, Shravasti in Kosala, and others. It would appear that the social and political backgrounds out of which the great philosophies and religions of the world are born are almost bound to have elements in common. Out of a condition of intellectual ferment and turmoil in one part of the world came the philosophy of Shakyamuni, which provided a dialectical resolution of the conflicting doctrines of the six teachers and the ninety-five Brahman sects, while out of a similar turmoil in another part of the world came the philosophy of Socrates.

THE YEARS
OF AUSTERITY

3

THE ENCOUNTER WITH KING BIMBISARA

Whether Shakyamuni, when he chose Magadha as the place to carry out his religious austerities, was aware of the existence there of the six non-Buddhist teachers discussed above we have no way of knowing, nor is there any record indicating that he met the six teachers during his stay there. Concerning these questions, we can only speculate on the basis of what is known of Shakyamuni's educational background.

Kapilavastu, Shakyamuni's native city, seems to have had rather good educational facilities, since it is said that some of the families of Kosala, the more powerful state upon which the Shakyas were dependent, sent their sons to Kapilavastu to receive instruction in the civil and military arts. It would appear that the Shakyas, though politically weak and obliged to place themselves under the protection of Kosala, were a proud and spirited people who held education in high esteem.

Though we are not told the name of any particular teacher from whom he received instruction as a student, Shakyamuni undoubtedly would have studied the teachings of Brahmanism. He may have studied at a regular school in the same manner as the sons of members of the Brahman class, or his father may have summoned Brahman teachers to the palace and had them instruct his son in one of the pleasure gardens that he had built for him. All we know is that, according to legend, the youthful Shakyamuni astounded his teachers with his broad learning and his rapid progress in letters and arithmetic.

Even in such an intellectual environment, it is unlikely that he could have had very detailed knowledge of the new cultural and philosophical movements that were arising in the state of Magadha. And yet, though on a smaller scale, the same types of movements must have been taking place in the nearby state of Kosala as well, and so one cannot help feeling that Shakyamuni, with his keen intelligence and sensitivity, must have sensed almost intuitively that there were new and powerful forces stirring in the world outside Kapilavastu. Vague rumors that had reached him during his studenthood concerning the new intellectual and spiritual currents may have come suddenly to his mind again when he attained adulthood and determined to embark upon the religious life, prompting him to turn his steps in the direction of Magadha.

Upon reaching Rajagriha, the capital of the state of Magadha, near which, incidentally, the Lotus Sutra was later preached, Shakyamuni must have wandered about the city and its environs observing the ways of life practiced by the various ascetics and religious leaders congregated there. It was in the course of these wanderings, we are told, that he was spotted by the keen eye of the ruler of Magadha, King Bimbisara.

According to tradition, the king, looking down from a palace tower at the large numbers of ascetics who were going about the city begging alms, noticed Shakyamuni and, realizing that he was no ordinary person, ordered his attendants to follow the young man. They did so, and after learning that Shakyamuni was living in the foothills of Mount Pandava to the west of the city, they returned and reported to the king. King Bimbisara, accompanied by his retinue, then went to the foothills in person to meet the future Buddha.

If this story is true, it suggests that there was something striking about Shakyamuni's appearance—perhaps a kind of indefinable luminosity—that drew the attention of the king. It also suggests that the king was a man of extraordinary perception to have singled out Shakyamuni in the crowd of religious mendicants. In fact, history strongly implies that this king was no ordinary leader. In a period when Indian society was undergoing a process of turbulent change and small tribal states were being swallowed up by their more powerful neighbors, King Bimbisara not only protected his state from danger but also strengthened it and greatly extended its sphere of influence.

When the king reached the foothills of Mount Pandava, he found Shakyamuni seated in repose. Approaching him without hesitation, the king said: "You are young in years, handsome in appearance, and seem to be of noble birth. I will give you all the wealth you desire. My elephant battalions and the finest and bravest troops of my army are at your command."

The king then asked where Shakyamuni had been born. The latter replied that he was a prince of the kingdom of the Shakyas, which was under the hegemony of Kosala.

In response to the king's offer of riches and the command of his armies, Shakyamuni replied: "I have left my home and family and have no desire for worldly things. Worldly desires bring many entanglements, and only when one is free from them can one find peace and rest. Knowing this, I have embarked upon the ascetic life in order to seek the truth. This alone is my objective—I desire nothing else."

This passage, which derives from one of the oldest works in the Buddhist canon, helps to explain the deep impression Shakyamuni made on the king, inspiring the latter to offer riches and the command of his army to the young man. Like any competent political leader in any country, King Bimbisara must have been constantly on the watch for men of unusual ability who could aid the future development of his state, and something in Shakyamuni's bearing told him that he was in the presence of such a man. Some scholars have surmised that King Bimbisara, when he offered to place his armies at Shakyamuni's disposal, already knew that the young man was the crown prince of the Shakya kingdom, which was a dependent of Kosala, the chief rival of

the state of Magadha, and hoped in this way to draw the Shakya kingdom into his own sphere of political influence. However, there is no
reason to suspect that he had such an ulterior motive.

The scriptural account goes on to relate that after Shakyamuni
refused the king's offer, the king did not press him further. Instead, he
requested that, when Shakyamuni had achieved the enlightenment he
was seeking, he allow the king to become the first person to hear the
newfound truth. Indeed, we are told that after Shakyamuni achieved
enlightenment he did return to Magadha, though it was not the first
stop on his journey, and at that time King Bimbisara became one of
his followers.

King Bimbisara is mentioned in various Buddhist scriptures, so
his name is familiar to followers of Buddhism. In spite of his earlier
glory, however, his last years seem to have been unfortunate, for we are
told that his son Ajatashatru rose up in rebellion against him, imprisoned him, and eventually put him to death. Perhaps by that time he
had already fulfilled his mission in life, though one cannot help being
moved to reflection by the severity of the blow dealt him by fate.

~

THE TWO BRAHMAN HERMITS

According to scriptural accounts, after his meeting with King Bimbisara at the foot of Mount Pandava, Shakyamuni selected two hermit-
sages from among the large number of ascetics in the area and began
his religious practices under them. These sages were Alara Kalama and
Uddaka Ramaputta.

The recluse or hermit-sage is a familiar figure in Asian religions.
In China, such recluses are often depicted as having the power to fly
through the air and perform other unusual feats and were regarded as
the ideal of the Taoist religion. In India, from Brahmanic times on, we
find examples of men who lived in the seclusion of the mountains or

the forest, sought religious enlightenment, and were noted for their virtue. Such hermit-sages were regarded as the highest authorities in matters pertaining to the Brahman religion, and it was from among men of this type that Shakyamuni chose his two teachers.

After arriving in Magadha, Shakyamuni no doubt heard much about the so-called six non-Buddhist teachers mentioned earlier, though whether he ever actually met any of them is not known. But, perhaps because the radical nature of their thought and religious practices in some sense repelled him, he turned instead to two men of a very different type. One can only guess why he chose these particular men to be his teachers, but I would suggest that it was probably because both were masters of yogic meditation. Alara Kalama was said to have reached the stage known as "the realm of nothingness" through meditation, while Uddaka Ramaputta had attained "the realm of neither thought nor no thought."

Such yogic meditation, along with various ascetic practices, was held in high esteem in ancient India. Yoga probably originated among people who, as the third phase of their past life, had retired to the seclusion of the forest and were reflecting upon their past life. By Shakyamuni's time, however, it had come to have a more specifically philosophical and religious significance. That is, it was practiced with the aim of attaining not only concentration of the mind and introspection into one's inner being but actual emancipation from the body through psychic control.

In Brahmanism, and particularly in the philosophy of the Upanishads, spirit and matter are regarded in dualistic terms and are therefore seen as opposed to each other. It is from this opposition of body and spirit, according to the Upanishads, that various misfortunes and sufferings are engendered. To overcome this opposition, people must accelerate the workings of the pure and undefiled spirit with which they were originally born until it has absorbed within itself all the material elements of being. This was what yogic meditation taught one to do, and in Shakyamuni's time, it was widely practiced among ascetics as a form of religious discipline.

In the more materially advanced countries of the world today, there is considerable interest in the meditative practices of yoga and Zen as ways of dealing with the spiritual desolation of the times, and there may likewise have been those in Shakyamuni's age who looked to yoga for the same reason. A more fundamental reason for the popularity of yoga practice in Shakyamuni's time was that it was regarded as a means of gaining deliverance from the sufferings attendant upon the human condition.

This concept of emancipation, expressed by the word *vimukti* in Sanskrit and *gedatsu* in Japanese, is a characteristically Asian one. Its closest equivalent in the West would probably be the concept of freedom, yet emancipation and freedom are not the same thing. Freedom in the Western sense is always seen in the context of the institutional principles of human society. But freedom in the Eastern sense means freedom from the sufferings that are inherent in human existence, regardless of the social institutions that may prevail.

Considering this matter globally and historically, in the past the East has perhaps been too deeply involved in the effort to attain deliverance from the fundamental human condition, and in doing so has tended to neglect the problems of society. The Western concept of freedom, by contrast, being a quest for the rights of a person as a social being, has brought about a number of changes and improvements in the institutions of society. Indeed, it may be regarded as one of the factors leading to Western civilization's dominance over the spiritual civilization of the East in recent centuries. We must try to understand and appreciate both concepts of freedom, however, without expending undue time on the question of which is superior. I would only note that, in view of the conditions faced by the world today, I believe it is the Eastern concept of emancipation that is needed now.

In any event, in his day it was quite natural that Shakyamuni, who

had set out to solve the great problems posed by human sickness, suffering, and death, should have been attracted to the hermits and their
methods of yogic meditation. He first studied under Alara Kalama,
who is reported to have had some three hundred disciples. It is not
certain where his hermitage was located, some sources placing it in
Vaishali, a city located a short distance from Magadha, others in the
Vindhya Mountains.

As noted earlier, Alara Kalama was said to have achieved "the realm
of nothingness," while Uddaka Ramaputta had attained that known as
"the realm of neither thought nor no thought." These states of *samadhi*, or concentration, were later incorporated into Buddhist methods of meditation and discipline. But in the ten stages of advancement
toward Buddhahood, they occupy a relatively low position, the former
corresponding to the stage of voice-hearer (*shravaka*), one who hears
the doctrine and understands it only theoretically, and the latter to
that of the *pratyekabuddha*, or "cause-awakened one," one who com-
prehends the nature of the enlightened mind but is interested only in
his own salvation. Hence, they are below the stage of the bodhisattva,
who vows to save all humankind, or that attained by Shakyamuni himself. Shakyamuni realized very quickly that these states of *samadhi* were
not his ultimate goal.

In the sutra known as the Medium-Length Agama Sutra (one of
the four Agama sutras), it is recorded that Shakyamuni astonished
his teacher Alara Kalama by the rapidity with which he attained "the
realm of nothingness," that is, the state of emptiness in which one is
free from all worldly attachments. The latter suggested that hence-
forth they share the work of teaching the disciples. Shakyamuni, however, declined the offer and took leave of Alara Kalama, saying, "This
teaching does not lead to philosophical seclusion, to the stifling of the
passions, to cessation, to tranquility, to supreme awakening, or to Nirvana, but only to the realm of nothingness.'"

The object of Shakyamuni's search was the kind of enlightenment that would set humanity free from the sufferings involved in the round of birth and death. But the method expounded by Alara Kalama fell far short of this goal. Emancipation from attachment to worldly things was only part of the ultimate truth, Shakyamuni realized, and for this reason he left the hermitage.

Much the same thing happened, according to the Medium-Length Agama Sutra, when Shakyamuni went to study under the hermit Uddaka Ramaputta, who is said to have lived near the city of Rajagriha in Magadha and to have had seven hundred disciples. Shakyamuni very soon reached the same level of *samadhi* as his teacher, "the realm of neither thought nor no thought." But, realizing that this, too, failed to lead to the kind of enlightenment he was seeking, he left this hermitage as well.

It is difficult to say exactly what is meant by "the realm of neither thought nor no thought." So long as one has thoughts or ideas, he is still moving within the realm of conceptualization. But true enlightenment must somehow break free of the shell of conceptualization and seize upon the essence of life itself. At the same time, what succeeds in seizing upon that essence is one's own thinking self, and perhaps this is why the stage is described as possessing "neither thought nor no thought." What is important to note is that Shakyamuni studied under these two teachers, both regarded as the greatest masters of yoga practice of the time, and attained a level of achievement equal to that of his mentors. Realizing that such methods would not lead him to his goal, however, he abandoned them and turned to the practice of various austerities.

For yoga masters like Alara Kalama and Uddaka Ramaputta, yoga practice had become an end in itself, and they had apparently forgotten the ultimate objective for which one adopts such practices, that of attaining enlightenment. The same thing can perhaps be said of some of the more superficial followers of meditation-based disciplines today. They feel that it is sufficient merely to sit in meditation and still their minds. If one were inclined to speak unkindly of them, it could be said that they are in danger of mistaking what is really nothing more than a foggy state of mind for some lofty level of spiritual achievement. Both yoga and Zen meditation are excellent practices developed by Asian philosophy and religion, but, as Shakyamuni made clear, they should be employed as methods for attaining an understanding of the ultimate truth, not looked upon as ends in themselves.

THE PRACTICE OF AUSTERITIES

Convinced that he could not attain the enlightenment he was seeking under the two yoga masters, Shakyamuni decided to devote himself to the practice of austerities. According to some accounts, he pursued this life for six years; according to other accounts, for ten. He conducted these practices in a forest near the village of Sena in the Uruvilva district, a little west of the city of Rajagriha. This village is said to have been situated on the Nairanjana, a tributary of the Ganges; Buddhagaya, the place where Shakyamuni eventually attained enlightenment, is situated along the same river.

In one of the scriptures, Shakyamuni offers the following vivid description of the surroundings in which he carried out his austerities: "Thus seeking after good and in quest of the way to an incomparable state of peace, I came, in the course of my wanderings through Magadha, to the village of Sena in Uruvilva, and there took up my abode. It was a delightful place, with the clear waters of the Nairanjana flowing through a rich and fertile land. Little villages drowsed in the shade of splendid trees along lovely banks and ghats, and meadows stretched away into the distance. As I surveyed the place, I thought to myself, 'It is an inviting spot for a young man of good family who is set on striving.' So I sat down and said to myself, 'This is indeed a place propitious for ascetic practice.'"

The forest outside the village of Sena was a gathering place for Brahmans who had left their families and were practicing austerities. Like yogic meditation, the practice of austerities was regarded in Indian philosophy as a method of attaining spiritual advancement and was widely resorted to. Underlying it were the same concepts of the duality of mind and matter and the search for emancipation discussed above. By subjecting the body to various painful processes and learning to endure the pain and suffering that resulted, it was believed, one could acquire spiritual freedom.

The various austerities practiced in Shakyamuni's day have been classified into four categories: control of the mind, suspension of breathing, total fasting, and severe dietary restriction. These disciplines were carried out in strict obedience to detailed sets of rules. In the discipline designed to control the mind, for example, one seats oneself in a formal posture, clenches the teeth lightly, presses the tongue against the upper palate, and in this position concentrates upon bringing the mind under total control. This sounds relatively straightforward, but when continued for hours at a time, it is said that breathing becomes increasingly difficult and sweat pours from the armpits.

The exercise designed to achieve suspension of breath is regarded as one of the most difficult. First, one concentrates upon preventing breath from passing in and out through the nose or mouth. One might suppose that this would lead to suffocation, but when breathing through the nose and mouth is suspended, according to yogic authorities, one starts "breathing through the ears." This is said to lead to a severe ringing of the ears and to be almost unbearably painful. If one advances to the point of arresting the breath in and out of the mouth and nose, one then proceeds to arrest the breath passing through the ears, which results in violent pains in the head, and goes on to arrest the breath passing through the abdomen, and so on for all the other parts of the body.

As for fasting, fasts that last from twenty-four hours to a week are regarded as appropriate only for beginners. More advanced followers of the discipline customarily fast for one month, two months, or even as long as six months in succession. The fasts observed by the followers of the Jain religion are famous for their severity. According to some accounts, nine of the eleven disciples of Nigantha Nataputta, the founder of Jainism, fasted to death, and it is believed that by doing so they attained final deliverance.

Reading descriptions of such painful and inhuman practices, one realizes anew what frightening consequences can ensue when a religion or ideology is carried to an extreme. And yet, as in the case of the Jains, although the practices themselves may seem harsh and extreme, they are not without philosophical significance in their intent.

The term for such austerities in Sanskrit is *tapas*, which literally means "heat." This word referred originally to a practice in which one sat or stood naked in the heat of the burning sun until one's flesh was scorched and seared. As stated earlier, the body was believed to be defiled while the spirit was basically pure, and it was therefore only after one had subjected the flesh to mortification that the spirit could attain the kind of peace that represented final emancipation. Such austerities were regarded as an important method to be used in the search for enlightenment, and it was traditionally believed that any person who had left his family and entered the religious life must necessarily at some point devote himself to such practices before he could hope to reach the heart of the ultimate truth.

Consequently, in order to attain the enlightenment that he could not find through yoga meditation, Shakyamuni must have felt that he had no alternative but to devote himself to the practice of austerities. No one can step out of one's own age, and Shakyamuni, like others of his time, believed that unless he tasted the pain and bitterness of such practices, there was no hope of true spiritual advancement.

I wonder if the same cannot be said for all who grasp some great truth or make discoveries that change the course of history. The kind of wisdom that allows one to become a leader, commanding the attention of an entire age, is never born from practices that are simple and easy. Shakyamuni, too, I believe, thought that only by undergoing the experience of suffering involved in such disciplines and by confronting them face to face could he achieve any unique discovery of his own.

Unless we adopt some such interpretation, it is difficult to account for the fact that more than half the period during which Shakyamuni was searching for enlightenment was occupied by such practices: ten years according to one account, as we have seen, or six years according to another. Particularly in matters of religion and ideology, one cannot hope to grasp the essence of a thing unless one enters into it and experiences it directly.

Today we are accustomed to the scientific spirit, with its strong tendency to apply objective standards of measurement and to view things from the outside. But the search for true enlightenment allows for no such bystander's approach; advancement in most cases can only be achieved by the process of direct, firsthand experience.

In Shakyamuni's case, we may be certain that when he entered the forest outside the village of Sena, he practiced various types of austerities in an earnest and thoroughgoing manner. The scriptures record that those around him were astonished by the severity of the practices that he undertook, and at one point even believed that he had died as a result. In his later years, when he was recalling this period of his life, he recollects that no Brahman or *shramana* ascetic in the past had ever undergone nor would any ever be likely to undergo—the kind of severe self-torture that he himself had endured, although he did not thereby gain enlightenment.

The note of self-assurance in this statement is important, for it indicates that he was convinced that he had entered into these ascetic practices determinedly and wholeheartedly and had persisted until he had penetrated into the very essence of such practices. When, failing to attain the goal that he sought, he later abandoned such practices, he did so not out of frustration or a failure of willpower but only after he had grasped the quintessence of asceticism and found it of no use to him. This is an important point, for it indicates that enlightenment in Buddhism is attained only by those passionate seekers who have gone through the most severe ordeals.

THE REJECTION OF AUSTERITIES

Shakyamuni studied yoga, especially the art of meditation, under two teachers, but after mastering their techniques he left them. Then, after practicing the most severe mortifications of the flesh, he gave up those practices as well and went his own way in the quest for supreme wisdom. These two acts of rejection are important, for they clearly indicate that Buddhism is not a teaching that advocates the practice of extreme asceticism, nor is it merely a meditative and idealistic philosophy. It is, rather, a religion based upon the assumption that fundamental truths can be explained in a commonsensical manner to each and every individual. In other words, it is the religion of the Middle Way that rejects both asceticism and hedonism as one-sided extremes.

In the Dharmachakra-pravartana Sutra, which records his first sermon following his enlightenment, Shakyamuni addresses the following words to his five disciples: "There are two extremes in this world, O Bhikkhus, which the religious wanderer should avoid. What are these two? The pursuit of desires and indulgence in sensual pleasure, which is base, low, depraved, ignoble, and unprofitable; and the pursuit after hardship and self-torture, which is painful, ignoble, and unprofitable.

"There is a middle way, O Bhikkhus, discovered by the Tathagata, which avoids these two extremes. It brings clear vision and insight, it makes for wisdom and leads to tranquility, awakening, enlightenment, and Nirvana...."

This may be taken as a kind of summing up by Shakyamuni of his life both as a prince and as an ascetic. He rejects as undesirable extremes both the luxurious life that he had lived in the palace and his severe ascetic practices. It offers an admirable summation of his philosophy and practice, which, in its rejection of both hedonism and asceticism, implies that mind and body are inseparable.

Hedonism and asceticism, although they are poles apart in most respects, share one characteristic: they are both products of dualistic thinking. The ascetics, for instance, viewed mind and body as two opposing substances, clearly to be distinguished from each other. The body is impure and evil; the spirit is pure and good. According to this way of thinking, only by destroying the body, or at least subjecting it to extreme mortification, can the spirit be set free. The teachings of the Jains are typical of such a viewpoint, and for this reason, when Jain followers fasted to the point of death, they were regarded as having attained nirvana.

If the body is the source of evil, there is no choice but to destroy it. This type of thinking has given rise to religions that teach that this world will always be impure so long as people continue to be burdened with bodies, and that only after death can people hope to reach the Pure Land or Paradise. It would appear that, generally speaking, dualism is always at work behind the dogmas of those religions that stress the concepts of a Pure Land or Paradise, Christianity not excepted.

Hedonism, needless to say, goes to the other extreme. Rejecting purity of spirit and life after death as mere figments of the imagination, it believes only in the existence of the body and matter and in the importance of trying, so far as possible, to satisfy all physical desires. In the eyes of the enlightened Buddha, of course, the views of both the hedonist and the ascetic represent biased and undesirable extremes.

The kind of self-denial found in extreme asceticism was perhaps most highly and systematically developed in ancient India, but we can find similar approaches in almost every age and area. Today much attention is focused upon the question of the human ego. Because the ego, or self, seems to be responsible for many of the problems that imperil our civilization, such as environmental pollution and the development of nuclear weapons, there is a tendency to regard it as intrinsically evil and to call for its denial.

Naturally, it is quite proper to be conscious of such problems, but to attempt to deny the self altogether seems to me an extreme. Rather, I think, one should try to grasp the entity called *ego* from the point of view of the life of humankind as a whole and attempt to determine the proper way in which it should be guided and directed.

The ideal of self-denial is often pure in motive and is something that any seeker of truth must at some point come to grips with. Even the Buddhist monk leading a homeless life may, in one sense be said to be practicing self-denial. The "human revolution" too, with its more distinctively modern, lay-centered approach to the Buddhist life, is a process whereby one challenges and comes to grips with the stern reality of self. But self-denial should never become an end in itself, for if it does, nothing constructive will ever result.

In Shakyamuni's day, asceticism tended to go to extremes because it was based upon dualistic thinking and a biased view of life and human nature. In the course of practicing austerities, Shakyamuni came to realize this clearly and therewith abandoned the practices that he had pursued for so long. In doing so, he took the first step toward the establishment of a new religion, one that was to be totally different from all religious traditions up to that time. In this sense, abandoning asceticism was a major turning point in his life, comparable in its significance to his earlier decision to leave his family and embark upon the religious life.

Once he had abandoned his practice of austerities, events apparently moved rapidly, and it was not long before he attained enlightenment. It is not known exactly how many days elapsed, but according to tradition, enlightenment came to him shortly after he left the forest where he had been practicing asceticism.

This forest was a gathering place for Brahman ascetics, so Shakyamuni could not have been alone while he was engaged in his practices.

Undoubtedly he learned the various methods to be followed from his fellow ascetics, though whether he studied under or attached himself to any particular ascetic we do not know. Legend states, however, that there were five ascetics who accompanied him, men who were so impressed by the severity of his discipline that they were convinced he would one day attain enlightenment. It was to these five ascetics, or *bhikkhus*, that Shakyamuni preached his first sermon, as we will see.

There are several theories as to how these men came to accompany Shakyamuni during the years when he was practicing austerities. According to one theory, they were Brahmans who were dispatched by Shakyamuni's father, because he was worried about his son's welfare. Another claims that they had no connection with the Shakya kingdom but decided to join Shakyamuni and live with him because they were impressed by his practice of austerities. Still another version claims that they were sent by Shakyamuni's father at a much later date, when he had heard rumors that his son was in danger of dying from the severity of his discipline and hoped thereby to prevent such a calamity. One of the ascetics bears a name that indicates that he was a native of the Shakya kingdom, and one therefore suspects that they were Brahmans who had a more-than-casual connection with Shakyamuni's native state.

Though these five *bhikkhus* had earlier been convinced that Shakyamuni would surely attain enlightenment through the practice of austerities, they lost all faith in him when he abandoned such practices and, declaring that Shakyamuni had "grown luxurious in his ways and given up the struggle," left him in disgust. This anecdote serves to illustrate the degree to which ascetic practices were respected among people devoting themselves to the religious life, and the great courage that Shakyamuni displayed in giving them up. But, possessing unwavering conviction and confidence, he ignored the accusations and slanders of those about him and proceeded calmly on his way toward enlightenment.

THE ENLIGHTENMENT   4

After practicing all of the most severe austerities known to his time and failing to gain enlightenment through them, Shakyamuni abandoned such practices. Shakyamuni's next step was to attempt to regain his strength, which had been greatly impaired by the privations he had endured. Buddhist sculptures representing Shakyamuni at this moment in his life portray in terrifying detail the wraithlike state of emaciation to which he had been reduced.

According to legend, when he gave up the life of austerity, Shakyamuni bathed in the Nairanjana River to wash off the dirt and filth that had collected on his body, though he was so weakened by his ordeals that he could barely climb back onto the bank of the river. This custom of bathing in a river to attain physical and spiritual purification is a characteristically Indian one and remains very popular to the present day.

The custom of purificatory bathing in rivers seems to have been widely practiced among the ascetics of Shakyamuni's time and probably is related in origin to the ancient Indian belief in nature deities that inhabit the rivers, trees, soil, and other natural objects. As for Shakyamuni's particular act of bathing, it is probably safe to assume that it symbolized his determination to end his ascetic practices and make a new start in his search for truth. Before proceeding with that search, he desired to purify both body and mind.

Shakyamuni then broke his long fast. The food he took, we are told, was a porridge or gruel made of rice boiled in milk, which was offered to him by a village girl named Sujata. There are various legends surrounding Sujata, one of which says that she was the daughter of the chief of Sena. It is not certain what motivated her to offer food to Shakyamuni, but all accounts agree that, nourished by the meal she offered him, he regained his strength and vitality and, filled with new vigor, soon won enlightenment.

Various sources identify the place where Shakyamuni gained enlightenment as the town of Gaya in Uruvilva, not far from the village of Sena. Because of this, it has come to be called Buddhagaya, and there is a temple there today. In similar fashion, the large tree under which Shakyamuni was seated when he gained enlightenment came to be called the *bodhi* tree, or tree of enlightenment. It was of the variety known as *ashvattha*, or pipal fig, which seems to have grown widely in various parts of India.

Meditating under a tree appears to have been a custom among the Indian ascetics of Shakyamuni's time. Buddhist scriptures and other writings make frequent mention of ascetics sitting in the quiet shade of a tree, practicing contemplation in hopes of grasping the nature of the inner self or of ultimate reality. The pipal tree in particular, with its widespread roots and luxuriant foliage, was from early times looked upon as holy and was regarded as providing a worthy place for the contemplation of immortality. It is not surprising, therefore, that Shakyamuni should have chosen this kind of tree to sit beneath when he embarked upon the last stage of his search for enlightenment. Even today in Buddhagaya, there is a large pipal or *bodhi* tree, though no claim is made that it is actually the tree under which Shakyamuni sat.

How he was attired when he took his place beneath the tree we do not know. Ascetics of that time are said to have often worn during their practices a shabby garment called a *pansukula*, which was made out of bits of old clothing that had been discarded in graveyards. Shakyamuni, too, may have worn such a garment, though this is pure conjecture. It is recorded that he took his seat upon a straw mat laid in the shade of the tree. Woven of soft *munja* grass, it was given to him as an offering by a farmer living nearby.

~

THE TEMPTATION OF MARA

So Shakyamuni seated himself on the mat under the pipal tree, determined to win enlightenment. He assumed the so-called lotus posture, which was the usual way of sitting in yogic meditation. In this posture the legs are crossed, with each foot placed sole-upward on the opposite thigh. The hands rest on the lap, the left over the right, palms upward and thumbs touching. This was regarded as the most stable and desirable position for sitting. The *Majaprajnaparamitapadesha*, a commentary by the great Buddhist philosopher Nagarjuna, who lived some six hundred years after Shakyamuni's death, praises this posture because it provides the greatest sense of firmness and stability, ensures that the hands and feet will be kept under control and the mind will not wander, and "fills King Mara with fear."

This last phrase brings us to the subject of the demon Mara, whom the scriptures describe in detailed accounts as tempting Shakyamuni while he sat under the *bodhi* tree. The temptation of Mara is a matter of great importance for the understanding of Buddhism, since Shakyamuni was said to have achieved enlightenment only after he had overcome the power of the demon leader and his army of followers. The whole process is known in Japanese Buddhism by the phrase *goma jodo*, or "conquering Mara and attaining Buddhahood."

According to the scriptures, Mara was alarmed at the prospect of Shakyamuni's triumph and said to the Buddha-to-be: "Emaciated and ashen of complexion, you are on the verge of death. Your chance of survival is one in a thousand. You ought to live, for only when alive it is possible for you to do good deeds.... However, your present efforts are vain and futile, for the way to the true dharma is hard, painful, and inaccessible." In this way, Mara first attempted to intimidate Shakyamuni, and when this failed, he turned to temptation.

This episode helps to reveal the true nature of what we call Mara, or devil king. Ordinarily, one tends to think of the devil as some kind of mysterious and supernatural being or perhaps merely as a kind of fairy-tale figure, but in Buddhism the concept of Mara is quite different. Mara is seen as a part of life that permeates the whole universe and, at the same time, as existing within the heart and mind of each individual. The true nature of Mara, as his standard epithet, "robber of life," reveals, is to work at all times to deprive human beings once and for all of their life force. In concrete terms, as seen in the passage from the scriptures quoted above, within a person who is advancing toward the goal of enlightenment and truth and exerting every effort to attain that goal, Mara is that which wells up and tries to block such attainment.

Buddhist philosophy speaks of the three obstacles and four devils. The four devils are (1) the hindrance of the five components, obstructions caused by one's physical and mental functions, (2) the hindrance of earthly desires, obstructions arising from the three poisons of greed, anger, and foolishness, (3) the hindrance of death, or an untimely death obstructing one's Buddhist practice, and (4) the hindrance of the devil king, who represents fundamental darkness, that is, the failure to comprehend the fundamental truth of human life.

But when these evil forces, Mara and his armies, appeared before Shakyamuni, he faced them squarely and would not give way an inch. Shakyamuni is said to have addressed Mara in the following words: "Friend of the slothful, Evil One, you have come here for your own sake. I have not the least need for merits. Mara should preach to those who are in need of merits. I have faith, heroism, and wisdom. Why do you ask me to live, I who am so intent?... As the flesh wastes away, my mind becomes more tranquil and firm. While I live thus, having attained the last sensation, my mind looks not to lusts.... Behold the purity of my being! Lusts are your first army, the second is called Aversion. Your third army is Hunger and Thirst, the fourth Craving. Your fifth is Sloth and Indolence, the sixth Cowardice. Your seventh army is Doubt, the eighth Hypocrisy and Stupidity. Gain, Fame, Honor, and Glory falsely obtained, the Lauding of oneself and Condemning of others. This is your army, Evil One. The coward does not overcome it, but he who overcomes it attains happiness. Wearing *munja* grass, I shall fight. Better to me is death in battle than that I should live defeated. Some ascetics and Brahmans plunged in this battle are vanquished: they know not the Way on which the virtuous, the good, go. Seeing the army on all sides, I go to meet Mara arrayed with elephants in the battle. He shall not drive me from my post."

In this way, we are told, Shakyamuni confronted and struggled fiercely with Mara.

Many would view this whole episode of the appearance of Mara and his armies as a late addition to the legend that is intended simply to lend a certain drama to the description of Shakyamuni's attainment of enlightenment. But it does more than that, I believe, for it reveals to us the true nature of Mara, or evil, in the world. Thus, we may interpret these passages dealing with Mara as descriptions of Shakyamuni's actual state of mind on the eve of his enlightenment and of the turmoil within him. If a person is to attain a state of great enlightenment, he must not be distracted and led astray by appealing enticements or his own petty desires. Only when he struggles against these forces within himself and concentrates all his efforts upon the attainment of his goal is there any hope of success. Therefore, although Mara is said to have "appeared before Shakyamuni," I believe we may take the episode as descriptive of something that in fact occurred within Shakyamuni's mind.

In the face of Shakyamuni's iron will and defiant posture, we are told, Mara finally gave up and withdrew with his army of followers, declaring: "For seven years I followed Shakyamuni step by step. I could find no entrance to the all-enlightened, the watchful one. Just as a crow went after a stone that looked like a lump of fat, mistaking it for a tender morsel, something sweet and delicious, and finding no sweetness there the crow departed: so like a crow attacking a rock, I leave Gautama in disgust and frustration."

Thus, after pursuing Shakyamuni for seven years, on the eve of Shakyamuni's enlightenment, Mara finally revealed his true form. Demons may be thought of as pervading the entire universe, but essentially they reside in people's minds. And only when we perceive them in their true form, as revealed within our own minds, can we strike at and destroy them. The appearance of Mara to Shakyamuni on the eve of his Buddhahood may be interpreted as Shakyamuni's perception of this truth; that is, he perceived in their true form the demons that existed within his own mind.

At times, the scriptures tell us, Mara appeared to Shakyamuni after he had attained enlightenment. The most famous instance took place when Shakyamuni, immersed in the joy of the newfound truth revealed by his enlightenment, was considering whether he should preach it to the world. At that point, Mara appeared to assail him with doubts. In the end, however, the deity Brahma pleaded with Shakyamuni to preach the dharma for the sake of humankind, and Shakyamuni gave his assent. In this case, the appearance of Mara with his doubts and of Brahma with his pleas may be taken to symbolize the process of hesitation and final resolution that went on in Shakyamuni's mind.

WHAT IS ENLIGHTENMENT?

After defeating Mara, Shakyamuni attained enlightenment. Tradition has it that this took place at the end of a night "in the full moon of Vaishakha." The full moon of Vaishakha occurs between April and May according to the solar calendar; therefore, in India, April 8 is often regarded as the date upon which this event took place. Owing to translational discrepancies and differences between cultures, however, in China and Japan, Shakyamuni's enlightenment is regarded as having taken place on December 8.

Whatever the exact day, Shakyamuni's enlightenment took place at dawn, "when the morning star appeared." Under the *bodhi* tree, he sat in deep meditation as the night wore on. With the approach of dawn, the eye of his wisdom gained sublime clarity, and when the morning star began to shine, he sensed his life bursting open and in a flash discerned the ultimate reality of things. In that moment, he became a Buddha, and the Buddhist faith, which was to have such an immeasurable impact upon the history of humankind, was born.

Just what was this state or condition of enlightenment that Shakyamuni attained? This is a difficult question to answer. To people of the present, the whole concept of enlightenment may seem strange and alien, but I do not think that it is a state that is very far removed from the experience of daily life. At the same time, it is all but impossible to explain in words. Even if it could be expressed in words, there are probably few people who could grasp and accept it immediately. Anyone who claimed to be able to do so would in fact have to be either a Buddha or a person of enormous conceit. Enlightenment is not something removed from or alien to ordinary human existence.

Buddhist philosophy describes the life that pervades the universe in terms of the Ten Worlds, each of which contains the other nine states, and of the "three thousand realms in a single moment of life." But it also says that exactly the same type of life is to be found within the mind of each individual. In Shakyamuni's case, as the darkness of night began to give way to the first light of dawn, the state of Buddhahood existing in the universe and the state of Buddhahood inherent in Shakyamuni's own life merged in harmonious communion and blossomed forth.

Thus, Shakyamuni's enlightenment was a kind of mutual response that took place between these two states of Buddhahood.

This kind of mutual response is not confined to the case of Shakyamuni. Jesus appears to have had a similar experience. Christ's enlightenment gave him his sense of mission and, therefore, in Buddhist terms, it represents a merging of the universal state of bodhisattva with the state of bodhisattva within his own mind, for the bodhisattva is the potential Buddha who vows to save all humanity before he himself enters Buddhahood.

We may go further and say that many great thinkers and people of genius have probably experienced enlightenment of one kind or another. Descartes, for example, on November 10, 1619, when he was absorbed in thought in a village on the Rhine, had a sudden flash of inspiration, according to his biographers, that revealed to him a "wonderful discovery" and a "marvelous science." The nineteenth-century existentialist philosopher Kierkegaard, while walking along lost in thought, is said to have had a sudden flash of understanding that shook his whole being.

In the West, such flashes of understanding are known as revelations and are traditionally believed to be imparted by a God who is absolute and omniscient. In terms of Buddhist philosophy, men like Descartes and Kierkegaard would be regarded as belonging to the category of *pratyekabuddha*, the level of existence just below that of Buddha and bodhisattva.

The *pratyekabuddha* is a being who, in the course of his own meditations and without relying upon others to teach him, gains a type of enlightenment. In a broad sense, any person of genius who, through his observations of natural phenomena, grasps some principle or makes some original discovery may be said to belong to this category of the cause-awakened one. Newton, who discovered the law of gravity after observing an apple fall from a tree, or Beethoven, who wrote the Pastoral Symphony after taking a walk in the countryside, are examples of people in this category.

All these people of genius were in a state of *samadhi*, or profound concentration, when they achieved their enlightenment or understanding. We will have more to say about this later; here I simply want to emphasize that enlightenment does not belong to a mystical level far removed from human experience and capability. Nevertheless, although the various men we have been discussing all attained a type of enlightenment, there is a qualitative difference between the enlightenment won by Shakyamuni and that attained by philosophers and people of intellectual genius. Such thinkers win a type of enlightenment in their respective fields of endeavor, but the truths that they discover are limited and fragmentary. They do not represent the kind of enlightenment that deals with ultimate reality and arises in response to the basic life force of the universe. This is where the essential difference lies.

However great the truths discovered by other thinkers of genius may be, they are not universal, profound, or fundamental enough to transform the destiny and suffering of the individual who apprehends them. Buddhahood, achieved through enlightenment, is the only state of life that can change a person's destiny and open up an infinite future. That is why Shakyamuni, having gained an understanding of truth, was totally committed to it for the remainder of his life. The enlightenment that he achieved was of the highest possible level.

THE CONTENT OF SHAKYAMUNI'S ENLIGHTENMENT

Thus, after many years of practicing austerities and after struggling with and overcoming Mara and his armies, Shakyamuni attained enlightenment. He was either thirty or thirty-five at the time he attained enlightenment, depending upon which account one accepts regarding the age at which he entered the religious life and the number of years he pursued it. Scriptures refer to his enlightenment by the Sanskrit term *anuttara-samyak-sambodhi*, which means "supreme perfect enlightenment," the kind that can perceive the true nature of all the manifold phenomena of existence. But what exactly was this unsurpassed wisdom? What was the essential nature of the world that Shakyamuni perceived that night under the *bodhi* tree in Buddhagaya?

The scriptures give various accounts of the content of Shakyamuni's enlightenment, but as we study each of these in turn, we are left in some confusion as to its exact nature. According to the Agama sutras, that enlightenment unfolded in three stages corresponding to the three watches of the night, and reached the stage of supreme perfect enlightenment during the third watch.

Prior to this, Shakyamuni is said to have gone through four stages of *dhyana*, or intense meditation. The first stage was reached by detaching himself from sense objects and passions. The second was marked by complete concentration of mind and a sense of joy. In the third stage, this sense of joy was transcended, and Shakyamuni retained only a feeling of serenity and peace. Finally, in the fourth stage, he attained a state of utter purity beyond all pain or delight, sorrow or joy.

These four stages of meditation were widely practiced among ascetics in Shakyamuni's time, and those who had mastered the third and fourth stages were looked upon as saints. For the Brahmans and other ascetics, these four stages were regarded as an end in themselves, and when one had mastered all four, he was thought to have reached the ultimate goal. In terms of the Buddhist concept of the threefold world —the world of desire, the world of form, and the world of formlessness—these four stages of meditation merely permitted one to shake off the delusions of the world of desire and enter the world of form; therefore, they did not represent true enlightenment. For this reason, Shakyamuni, after mastering them, proceeded to push ahead in his search for the supreme wisdom.

Having gained complete mastery over all four stages of meditation, his mind became clear, pure, undefiled, supple, and alert. He then entered upon the first watch of the night and the first stage of his true enlightenment. During this watch, we are told, he concentrated his mind on recollecting his previous existences. He recalled his first, second, and third lifetimes, and so on through countless aeons of time and countless formations and destructions of the universe; he recalled what his name had been in each existence, what he had eaten, what joys and sorrows he had known, what kind of death he had undergone, and how he had been reborn.

The passages in the scriptures that describe this process show us, in effect, that Shakyamuni had a clear vision of his life in all its manifestations throughout time. According to the doctrine of transmigration, which had from early times been expounded in Brahmanism, the life of a human being is by no means limited to the present. Shakyamuni, meditating under the *bodhi* tree, clearly recollected all of his previous existences one by one and perceived that his present existence was part of the unbroken chain of birth, death, and rebirth that had been continuing from incalculable aeons in the past. This was not something that came to him as a kind of intuition, nor did he perceive it as a concept or idea. It was a clear and real recollection—not unlike, though on a very different plane from, the events deeply buried within the recesses of our mind that we suddenly remember when we are in a state of extreme tension or concentration.

The Agama sutras end their description of Shakyamuni's enlightenment with the words, "Ignorance perished and gave way to insight." When Shakyamuni stamped out ignorance and acquired insight and wisdom, he could see with perfect clarity the realities of existence and the essential nature of this world.

The teachings of Shakyamuni comprise a staggering volume of literature and in later ages were referred to as the "eighty-four thousand teachings," but in the final analysis what Shakyamuni is saying is that so long as one is immersed in a life of ignorance, one will forever continue to be reborn in one or another of the six worlds, or states of existence, through which unenlightened beings continually pass. If one can acquire true insight and see the world with the wisdom of a Buddha, however, then one will surely experience the same bliss of enlightenment that the Buddha did and will achieve absolute happiness. "I myself have experienced this," Shakyamuni is saying, "therefore I want all of you to follow the same path."

After he had experienced the first stage of enlightenment, Shakyamuni proceeded to the second stage, that of the second watch of the night, during which he is said to have acquired wisdom regarding the future: "I acquired the supreme heavenly eye and beheld the entire world as if it were in a spotless mirror. I saw the passing away and rebirth of all creatures according to whether their acts were lower or higher. Those living beings whose acts are sinful pass to the sphere of misery; those others whose deeds are good win a place in the triple heaven. It became clear to me that no security can be found in this flood of *samsara*, and that the threat of death is ever present."

Shakyamuni apprehended the law of karma that governs the lives of all sentient beings throughout the past, present, and future. When perceived with eyes truly opened, all people are understood to transmigrate through the six paths of existence—those of hell, hungry spirits, animals, *asuras*, human beings, and heavenly beings. Moreover, this process is not limited to the present world but eternally repeats itself in the past and future as well. But humanity, enclosed in its little shell, does not face up to the reality of transmigration or to the severity of fate, perhaps because humanity is simply incapable of perceiving it, unequipped with the insight of a Buddha. What Shakyamuni did was survey with wisdom and clarity the death and rebirth of living beings everywhere. This, I believe, is how he passed the second watch of the night.

THE LAW OF CAUSATION

Having seen how living beings are destined to be constantly reborn in the worlds of the past, present, and future, Shakyamuni entered the final stage of his enlightenment in the third watch of the night. He apprehended the ultimate truth about life and the world, and thereby completed the process of becoming a Buddha. But what exactly was this final truth? The scriptures are in general agreement in their accounts concerning the first and second watches, but they differ considerably as to what Shakyamuni realized during the third watch. One scripture says that it was the twelve-linked chain of causation, while other sources identify it as the four noble truths or simply declare that he "attained sublime serenity and peace beyond old age, disease, death, anxiety, and defilements." Thus there is disagreement even among scholars concerning the nature of this last stage of enlightenment, though the general opinion seems to be that it concerned the law of causation.

The concept of causation, known in Sanskrit as *pratitya-samutpada,* or dependent origination, explains the fundamental process whereby all phenomena in the universe (including sentient beings) come into being as the result of causes. All things in the universe are subject to this law of cause and effect, and consequently nothing can exist independently of other things or arise of its own accord. For this reason, the theory of causation is often explained as either dependent origination or conditioned co-arising. This web of causation that binds all things is temporal as well as spatial, so that not only are all things in existence at the present moment dependent upon one another but all things existing in the past and future as well.

Scriptural accounts of the enlightenment of Shakyamuni contain the twelve-linked chain of causation, and followers of Theravada Buddhism seem to accept this formula as descriptive of Shakyamuni's insight concerning the law of causation. This may, however, be an oversimplification. Shakyamuni had set out upon the religious life in an effort to find a solution to the problems posed by birth, old age, sickness, and death. The concept of dependent origination that came to him at the moment of his enlightenment represents a universal law capable of solving those problems, but it is a law that is extremely profound in content and subtle in structure, and hence very difficult to explain in simple language. To provide something that would be easier for ordinary people to comprehend, he devised the formula known as the twelve-linked chain of causation.

The formula begins with the question, Why is man afflicted with old age and death? The twelve links in the chain, presented here in reverse order, proceed as follows: (12) Aging and dying are caused by birth, for without birth there would be no death. Then follows the question, How does birth arise? (11) Birth is caused by existence; (10) existence in turn is caused by attachment; (9) attachment is caused by desire; (8) desire is caused by sensation; (7) sensation is caused by contact; (6) contact is caused by the six sense organs; (5) the six sense organs are caused by name and form; (4) name and form are caused by consciousness; (3) consciousness is caused by karma; (2) and karma is caused by ignorance. (1) Ignorance is thus the ultimate link in the chain, the source from which all pain and suffering arise. If only ignorance can be wiped out, the links in the chain of causation will be broken one by one until aging and dying cease to exist. This is what Shakyamuni is saying.

I am inclined to take this formula as not much more than an expedient for preaching the truth that ignorance hinders man from achieving happiness. As a matter of fact, I do not believe that this doctrine, at least as it is expressed in this formula, represents the essence of the ultimate truth that Shakyamuni realized at the foot of the *bodhi* tree. That ultimate reality grasped by Shakyamuni can be better described, in my opinion, as the Law of Life, the world as it exists in a state of constant change.

When we look dispassionately at the great universe around us, we find that what at first glance appears to be a vast stillness is in fact constantly throbbing with creation and change. The same is true of human beings: They age, die, are reborn, and die again. Nothing, either in the world of nature or that of human society, knows a moment of stagnation or rest. All things in the universe are in flux, arising and ceasing, appearing and disappearing, caught in an unending cycle of change that is conditioned by the law of causation at work both temporally and spatially. Such is the nature of ultimate reality. My conviction is that Shakyamuni's enlightenment was a cry of wonder at the mysterious entity called life, whose myriad manifestations are joined to and dependent upon one another through the links of cause and effect.

But ordinary people are unaware of this truth and delude themselves into believing that they exist independently of one another. Such a delusion estranges them from the Law of Life, which is the ultimate truth, and causes them to become the prisoners of desire. From desires stem suffering, tragedy, and misfortune. Led astray by ignorance, which is a form of evil, there is no way out for them except to confront this evil that dwells in their minds.

Such, I believe, must have been the thoughts that passed through the mind of Shakyamuni, insofar as it is possible for an ordinary man like myself to guess. Having attained enlightenment, he himself was free of the ignorance that blinded other men and could live in accordance with the true Law of Life. What joy he must have felt! What Shakyamuni attained under the *bodhi* tree was an intuitive grasp of the essence of life. In the last analysis, the content of his enlightenment is the Law of Life itself.

If Shakyamuni had attempted to teach this Law of Life, however, with its highly intricate structure and wealth of philosophical subtleties, ordinary people would not have understood him. He was aware of the need to make the Law accessible to all common mortals, who were still victims of pain and suffering. First, he had to teach them the way to cure their suffering. It was then that Shakyamuni appeared before humanity like a superb physician and preached various laws or doctrines according to the symptoms displayed by his patients. These teachings, along with the explications and commentaries appended to them by his followers, in time grew into the so-called eighty-four thousand teachings.

SHAKYAMUNI
THE TEACHER

5

THE DECISION TO PROPAGATE THE LAW

After attaining enlightenment, Shakyamuni devoted the remaining years of his life to preaching the dharma, or Law, thus introducing a new religion to the world. But as we have seen above, he hesitated for a time before deciding to propagate the Law. According to some accounts, though Shakyamuni strove hard during his years of study and ascetic practice and in the end attained enlightenment, the salvation of humankind was not his initial aim, and he was of two minds as to whether he should preach the Law to others. This view seems to contradict the generally accepted theory that he renounced his royal home in order to seek salvation for all humankind.

The Agama sutras, in their description of the enlightenment, record that Shakyamuni sat for some time simply savoring the bliss of understanding. Then he became deeply perturbed as to whether he should reveal his newly won wisdom to others. It was at this point that Mara and Brahma made their appearances. The tendency within his own being that told Shakyamuni it was not necessary to preach the Law appeared to him in the shape of Mara, but he overcame and dispelled this apparition. The altruistic determination to share his enlightenment with all people welled up within him, and this is what the scriptures represent as the pleading of Brahma.

My own feeling is that Shakyamuni gave up his home and family not so much for the conscious purpose of saving humankind but with the hope of finding some solid and fundamental principle of truth. This happens with many people, does it not? They embark on what at first is meant to be a pure and disinterested search for truth, but in the course of searching they suddenly find themselves in possession of some major law or principle of life. As a result, they become aware of their own mission, spend the remainder of their lives proclaiming this new principle with all their energy, and leave behind them a name as a great religious leader or thinker. This is the pattern that Shakyamuni's life followed.

It would be going too far, however, to say that in the beginning he had no thought whatsoever of the salvation of humanity. After all, the very act of leaving his family and entering upon the religious life shows that he felt anguish over the sufferings of humanity, and his impassioned attempts to find a solution to these problems already point toward a desire for universal salvation.

Some scholars, viewing this stage in Shakyamuni's life and attempting to analyze it in terms of the Ten Worlds, or ten states of human existence, would say that when Shakyamuni was still seated in the initial bliss of his enlightenment, he was in the realm of the *pratyekabuddha*, the being who achieves enlightenment through his own efforts, and that when he resolved to propagate the Law, he then entered the realm of the bodhisattva.

It is more common, however, to classify him as a bodhisattva during the period when he had left his family and was engaged in the practice of severe asceticism, and as a Buddha after he gained perfect wisdom. The former view probably represents a reflection of Mahayana Buddhist thought, which places great emphasis upon the figure of the bodhisattva and the importance of religious practice. It is not enough simply to gain an understanding of the Law; the important thing is to put it into practice by attempting to save others. That is why, in this view, when Shakyamuni determined to propagate the Law, he advanced from the state of *pratyekabuddha* to that of bodhisattva.

The Buddhist scholar Fumio Masutani described Shakyamuni's hesitation as to whether to preach the Law as stemming from "the solitude of the truly enlightened." The Law was known only to himself; no one else was aware of it. And if he were to try to expound it, ordinary people would have a difficult time understanding and accepting his words. Shakyamuni—sensing the tremendous gap between the radiant world of wisdom within himself and the deluded state of humanity—was assailed by a feeling of solitude and isolation. This is why he hesitated.

The enlightened person has sufferings known only to him- or herself, alone aware of the wisdom achieved. All the great pioneers and teachers in history have experienced this problem. The lion-like person is always lonely, because he or she alone understands the truth and his or her mission to expound it. Only when that person rises up in determination to tell the world of the truth that is within will this sense of loneliness be dispelled.

TURNING THE WHEEL OF THE LAW

A month or more seems to have elapsed between the time when Shakyamuni gained enlightenment and when he preached his first sermon at Sarnath, near the city of Varanasi. Varanasi is about 130 miles from Buddhagaya, where Shakyamuni achieved enlightenment. One can make the journey in around four hours by train today. However, it must have taken Shakyamuni more than ten days on foot.

Shakyamuni chose Varanasi rather than Magadha as the site of his first sermon, we are told, because he wished to preach to the five *bhikkhus*, or ascetics, with whom he had earlier practiced austerities and who were now living in Varanasi. These five men, it will be recalled, had been deeply impressed by the severity of the ascetic practices that Shakyamuni undertook and had predicted that he would surely attain enlightenment. When Shakyamuni abandoned such practices and began to take food again, however, they berated him for his "luxurious ways" and left the village of Sena.

We are not told why the five ascetics went to Varanasi after leaving Sena. Presumably, just as Magadha was famed as a gathering place for thinkers with new and original ideas, so Varanasi must have been regarded as a place endowed with an especially potent religious and philosophical atmosphere. The place in Sarnath, outside Varanasi, where Shakyamuni delivered his first sermon is known as the Deer Park because of the deer that wandered about freely. In Eastern thought, deer are commonly believed to gather about people of saintly character, and we can imagine that the Deer Park was particularly favored by people of strong religious leanings.

In any event, Shakyamuni learned that his five ascetic friends had settled there, and he determined to journey to Varanasi and preach to them. He knew them well from the years they had pursued the ascetic life together, and no doubt he wanted first of all to share his newly found enlightenment with them. It has also been suggested that Shakyamuni felt he would have greater success in spreading his teachings if he first made converts among men who were already devoted to the religious life rather than attempting to take his message directly to the masses. But a simpler explanation may be that he realized that, no matter what splendid concepts he might have in his mind, if he could not explain them in such a way as to convince people with whom he was already thoroughly familiar, he would never be able to teach the truth to people in general.

I find it an indication of his compassionate humanity that he should have chosen his old comrades to be the first to hear him preach. Nevertheless, when Shakyamuni appeared before them to preach his first sermon, he was greeted with some coolness. "Here comes our pleasure-loving friend Gautama, who gave up his austerities in favor of luxury," they must have said among themselves. "We must not get up to meet him."

The scriptures record that when he actually drew near them, however, they wavered in their original resolve and in fact greeted him with a considerable show of respect. They were convinced, nevertheless, that he had not attained true enlightenment, and they addressed him in familiar language. Shakyamuni is said to have reprimanded them for employing such forms of address to a *tathagata*, or Thus Come One, a title that refers to one who has arrived at a state of perfect enlightenment.

He then announced that, since he had attained perfect wisdom, they were to give ear to his teachings. His friends, however, were unconvinced. On the contrary, they asked whether anyone who had abandoned his earlier practice of religious austerities to live in comfort could possibly be expected to attain perfect wisdom. Shakyamuni reasserted his claim and announced that he was going to preach the Law to them, but they continued to offer objections. Finally, to put an end to the argument, he asked if they had ever seen him so radiant and resplendent or if they had ever known him to speak in this way before. In the end they acquiesced and agreed to listen to his teachings.

Apparently there was an air of confidence and authority in Shakyamuni's appearance and behavior that finally awakened the five ascetics and persuaded them that they should heed his words. It is significant to note, however, that though they listened to his teachings, they by no means gave immediate assent to them.

It is said that Shakyamuni and his five friends embarked upon a communal life at Sarnath, Shakyamuni preaching the Law to two or three of the ascetics while the others went about begging alms for the support of the group. They were, by this time, sufficiently intrigued to receive instruction but some interval was required before they could fully comprehend his teachings.

After considerable time spent in this communal life, Kaundinya acquired insight that allowed him to comprehend Shakyamuni's teachings, and he thus became the Buddha's first true disciple. Soon, one by one, the other four attained clarity and wisdom as well, and in this way the *sangha*, or Buddhist Order, was formed.

What exactly was the content of the dharma, or Law, that Shakyamuni preached to his first followers? It is generally asserted that he began by explaining the Middle Way, urging the rejection of both extreme hedonism and extreme asceticism. After he had made his position clear on this point, he proceeded to teach the four noble truths and the eightfold path. There is a great deal of controversy among scholars concerning the reliability of this account, however, some claiming that only the eightfold path was taught, others that the Buddha's initial teachings consisted of the four noble truths, and that the Middle Way and the eightfold path were added much later.

We can only guess as to which theory is correct. It is safe to conjecture, however, that after gaining enlightenment under the *bodhi* tree, Shakyamuni labored long and conscientiously over the precise form in which he would first present his teachings to the world. To explain the realm of supreme and mysterious wisdom in such a way that it would be comprehensible to others, he had to bring his explanations down to a more popular level and translate the principles of enlightenment into terms that could be generally understood and embraced.

If we accept the hypothesis that what Shakyamuni taught first was the four noble truths, we should note immediately that these represent a very realistic and practical doctrine. They begin by defining the problem, declaring that (1) all existence is suffering and that (2) suffering is caused by selfish craving. They then proceed to present the solution to the problem of suffering, asserting that (3) selfish craving can be destroyed and that (4) it can be destroyed by following the eightfold path.

The eightfold path is likewise an extremely clear and concrete list of principles to be followed in order to gain deliverance—namely, the observance of (1) right views, (2) right thinking, (3) right speech,

(4) right action, (5) right way of life, (6) right endeavor, (7) right mindfulness, and (8) right meditation.

Because of the extremely simple and practical nature of these doctrines, the five ascetics were able to understand them with relative ease. It is for the same reason that followers of Mahayana Buddhism regard these early doctrines (along with the Agama sutras that record them) as forms of the Law that have been adapted to the level of understanding of ordinary people and designed to entice them in the direction of an understanding of the higher principles of the Law. That would mean that this first sermon is less an approximation of the essence of Shakyamuni's enlightenment than a simple program for religious practice intended to lead people toward that enlightenment.

The Tiantai school of Chinese Buddhism, which later divided the teachings of the Buddha into five periods, may help to explain the philosophical distance that seems to exist between the essence of Shakyamuni's enlightenment and the practical doctrines that he preached in his first sermon at Sarnath. According to the Tiantai classification, the first sermon was delivered not at Sarnath but at Buddhagaya, where Shakyamuni had attained enlightenment. This first sermon consisted of the Flower Garland Sutra, a lofty work that closely reflects the true essence of the Buddha's enlightenment.

Shakyamuni's listeners, however, failed to understand what he was saying, and for that reason when he went to Sarnath, he preached the Agama sutras instead. According to Tiantai belief, these two occasions represent the first two of the five periods of the Buddha's teachings, the remaining three being the *vaipulya* period, when most of the Mahayana sutras were taught, and the periods during which he taught the Wisdom sutras and the Lotus Sutra, respectively.

Although there is very little historical evidence to support this theory, there is a certain logic to it. When Shakyamuni first made up his mind to preach the Law, he must have considered various ways in which to present the content of his enlightenment to the world at large. To that end he may well have devised, as one possible approach, the intricate system of thought expounded in the Flower Garland Sutra. But when he found that the Flower Garland Sutra, with its abstruse doctrine of the essential interdependence of all things in the realm of cosmic law, was unintelligible to the common person, he may have decided to try something of a simpler and more practical nature. The doctrines of the Agama sutras, with their strong ethical and practical element, represent his second attempt at a solution.

But let us leave these conjectures and return to the subject of the first sermon, which is generally accepted as having been delivered at Sarnath. It was in effect an announcement to the world of the birth of a new religion, and as such is often referred to as the first turning of the wheel of the Law.

The "wheel" in this expression derives from that possessed by a wheel-turning king, the symbol of an ideal ruler in Indian mythology. The term *turning of the wheel of the Law* derives from this concept and denotes the preaching of the highest truths of the universe by the Buddha, the supremely enlightened being. The ideal of the chakravartin, or wheel-turning king, derives from the same concept. I wonder if the phrase *turning the wheel* does not also in a sense symbolize the advent of a new era or a new society. Certainly, with the appearance of Shakyamuni and the truths concerning human existence that he taught, a new era in the history of philosophy and religion was born.

SHAKYAMUNI'S DISCIPLES

After the preaching of the first sermon and the conversion of the five ascetics, how did the new faith fare? All accounts indicate that it grew and spread at an impressive rate, and some claim that, within several years, Shakyamuni's followers numbered more than one thousand.

There are several factors that help to explain this rapid growth. In ancient India, the kind of individualism we take for granted in society today was unknown, and therefore if the father or grown son of a family converted to Buddhism, his entire family would customarily follow suit and join the faith as well. In addition, the Indian people, as we have seen, have characteristically shown deep interest in religion and philosophy, particularly during the period under discussion, so that when a young man became a disciple of Shakyamuni, his friends and acquaintances, out of natural curiosity, would go and listen to Shakyamuni's sermons for themselves. Because of these factors, Shakyamuni's early converts came to include royal families, such as that of King Bimbisara, and merchant families, such as that of the rich man Sudatta.

After converting the five ascetics, Shakyamuni and his newly won disciples remained for a time in Varanasi, the capital of the powerful kingdom of Kashi, located northwest of Magadha in central India. Prospering as a commercial city, it was situated at a strategic point commanding transportation routes by land and water and thus maintaining lively trade relations with other states.

Like Rajagriha, the capital of Magadha, Varanasi seems to have fostered a new class of wealthy merchants. In fact, Shakyamuni's first convert after the five ascetics was Yashas, the son of a rich merchant of Varanasi.

The story of Yashas's conversion is an interesting one and holds great significance for us today, illustrating that material wealth alone cannot satisfy one's spiritual needs. Yashas's life before his conversion is described in the same kind of symbolic terms as those employed to describe the early life of Shakyamuni. Brought up in surroundings of great luxury, he had three houses, one for use during the rainy season, one for the summer, and one for the winter. Constantly waited upon by female attendants, he spent his days feasting and being entertained by music and dancing.

Yet, despite of such delightful surroundings, he was ill at ease, for he had become disenchanted with his life of sensual indulgence, and the more merriment that went on about him, the deeper grew his feelings of emptiness and despair. Finally, one night he slipped away from his home and began wandering about in search of spiritual peace. It was then that he chanced to meet Shakyamuni.

Shakyamuni was resting at Sarnath when he heard the young man crying out in anguish. He called him to his side, assuring him that he would have no more cause for anguish, and began to preach the Law to him. Yashas, who until then had known only spiritual emptiness, responded to Shakyamuni's words with joy and converted to the new religion.

The truth that Shakyamuni preached to Yashas seems to have been based upon the law of karma, or causality, regarded in India as a matter of common sense, and the necessity of escaping from the cycle of birth and death. Judging from this, it would seem that Shakyamuni taught according to the needs and capacities of his listeners, making use of the generally accepted philosophical views and teaching people the proper way to live in terms of the law of causation.

He did not totally repudiate the Upanishadic philosophy, which at that time was the dominant religious thought of India, but made use of the widely accepted ideas of the Upanishads in expounding his own doctrine. He wished to guide people into the practice of Buddhism by presenting his teachings in as clear and reasonable a fashion as possible, one that would have the greatest general appeal.

There were, however, occasions when it became necessary for him to make clear certain fundamental doctrinal differences that existed between his Law and the Upanishadic philosophy. The great Buddhist philosopher Nagarjuna classified Shakyamuni's preaching methods into four ways or types. The first way is to preach to people in secular terms, explaining that Buddhism will fulfill their desires; the second is to preach according to people's respective capacities, thus enabling them to increase their store of good karma; the third is to help people abandon their illusions and free themselves from the three poisons of greed, anger, and foolishness; and the fourth is to reveal the ultimate truth directly, causing people to realize it.

During the forty-five or fifty years of his ministry, Shakyamuni must have had many occasions to use all four of these ways of preaching. In the case of Yashas, it would appear that Shakyamuni adopted the first two methods, preaching in such a way as to meet the spiritual needs and desires of the young man and in accord with his intellectual capacities.

Yashas, as we have seen, was deeply moved by Shakyamuni's words and resolved to become a monk. His entry into the Buddhist Order thus brought the number of disciples to six. But this does not end the episode concerning Yashas. We are told that his father, anxious about his son's safety, came in search of him and, hearing Shakyamuni's teachings, was converted and became a lay believer. He subsequently invited Shakyamuni to his home so that he might preach to Yashas's mother and wife, and they in turn were converted. In addition, Yashas's friends, who had always admired him for his keen intelligence, came to visit him and to observe his new life as a monk, and, hearing Shakyamuni's teachings, they were all converted and entered the Order, bringing the number of additional converts to fifty-four in all.

The story of Yashas and his conversion illustrates what a profound effect the faith of one man of intelligence and spiritual depth can have upon his family and the other young people of his generation. It also indicates how the tiny group of followers gathered about Shakyamuni was beginning to grow into a religious community of some size.

Shakyamuni, having laid the foundations for a new religious organization, then left Varanasi and journeyed to Uruvilva, the district where he had attained enlightenment, embarking on what was to be an extensive tour to propagate the faith. It is important to note at this point that he did not take with him the community of some sixty or more followers that had gathered about him in Varanasi. Instead he ordered his disciples to set out one by one to travel to various regions and preach the Law, while he proceeded alone to Uruvilva. According to scriptural accounts, he advised his followers that, since they had achieved the highest form of enlightenment and for the sake of the peace and happiness of the world, it was now their duty to travel from region to region, spreading these superlative teachings and demonstrating the proper way to put them into practice. They were not to go in groups of two or three but alone, as he himself was going to Uruvilva, and to transmit the teachings to as many people as possible.

This, it seems to me, tells us something very important about the fundamental spirit of Buddhism and its strong emphasis upon practice. It was the mission and proper endeavor of these men who had received Shakyamuni's teachings and entered the Buddhist Order to propagate the Law to all people for the sake of the peace and happiness of the world. One might think that Shakyamuni was being rather severe toward his followers by sending them off one by one on preaching missions rather than allowing them to remain together as a group. But, after all, Buddhism is not simply a system of philosophy, nor is it a religion for those who merely wish to pass their time in a world of quiet meditation. Rather Buddhism teaches that once one has sought the Way and found understanding, he should make it his life's mission to spread the knowledge of the Way among others and reach out to all sentient beings. It is this active practice and propagation of the faith that constitutes the core of the Buddhist religion. This has always been true from Shakyamuni's time to the present day.

In addition, Shakyamuni's command to his disciples to go their ways alone rather than in groups of two or three indicates the importance that he attached to the ability of the believer to act with full self-discipline and control. In the practice of Buddhism, his emphasis was upon the active and positive rather than the merely passive. He did not wish his disciples to be simple recipients of the Law but forceful propagators of it. He wanted each one to teach the Law in his own way and on his own initiative so that he would not only spread the message to others but also acquire a deeper understanding and faith. This practice of traveling alone to spread the teaching illustrates more than anything else the degree to which Buddhism is characteristically a religion of practice.

~

PREACHING AT URUVILVA

Taking leave of his band of disciples, Shakyamuni set off alone for Uruvilva and what was to be one of the most important phases of his preaching career. Among the converts he made there were a number of ardent and influential followers who later contributed greatly to the growth of the Buddhist Order. They included King Bimbisara of Magadha as well as the famous disciples Shariputra, Maudgalyayana, Mahakashyapa, and the three brothers of the Kashyapa clan. This would seem to indicate that Shakyamuni's preaching efforts in Uruvilva met with considerable success, his new religious doctrines gaining rapid adherence among ascetics, seekers of the Way, and men of influence and position who had grown discontented with the conventional philosophy and religion of the time.

One of the most curious episodes from this chapter of Shakyamuni's life concerns his conversion of some thirty young couples when he was on his way to Uruvilva. According to the story, Shakyamuni was seated in the midst of a dense forest practicing meditation when the group chanced upon him. Most of the couples were married, but one consisted of a young bachelor and a prostitute. When the prostitute made off with the young man's possessions, the entire group set out in search of her and happened to meet the Buddha. After listening to their story, Shakyamuni is said to have admonished them, saying, "Rather than seek for a prostitute, wouldn't it be better to seek for your own true self?" He then proceeded to teach the Law to them, and all the couples were converted.

The episodes concerning the conversion of Yashas and of the thirty couples both have a characteristically Indian ring to them, bespeaking the degree to which thinkers, ascetics, and monks were traditionally respected in India. At the same time, they indicate the admirable way in which Shakyamuni availed himself of every possible opportunity to preach the Law. They also testify to the tremendous power of personal attraction he must have exerted upon those who came into contact with him.

Such adherents as Yashas and the thirty young couples were by no means the types who enter a religious order because they can find no other livelihood. Like many others among Shakyamuni's disciples, they came from a class that was both intellectually and economically above the common level. This does not mean, of course, that Shakyamuni himself took any notice of class distinctions. He seems to have treated all his followers impartially, regardless of race, caste, class, or economic status. And yet the fact that many people of intellectual distinction and prominent social position were attracted to him is an indication of the warmth and personal magnetism that he must have possessed and that accounted in part for his large and enthusiastic following.

After reaching his destination in Uruvilva, Shakyamuni is said to have sought a confrontation with the followers of Brahmanism, particularly the prestigious Kashyapa brothers, who belonged to the Jatila sect of Brahman ascetics. These brothers, named Uruvilva Kashyapa, Nadi Kashyapa, and Gaya Kashyapa, wore their hair bound up in Brahman fashion, performed religious ceremonies, wielded great influence in the area, and are said to have had followings of five hundred, three hundred, and two hundred disciples respectively. Because of the Kashyapa brothers' renown in the area, it is very likely that Shakyamuni heard of them when he first went to Uruvilva to enter the forest and practice austerities. But because they were worshipers of Agni, the Brahman god of fire, he probably felt that their teachings would not be pertinent to his search for truth and therefore had not joined their band of disciples.

Now, however, as an Enlightened One, he wished to confront them and refute their doctrines from the standpoint of Buddhist teaching. In this way, too, it has been suggested, he could convert not only individuals but whole sects of Brahman believers to his teachings and thus greatly facilitate the spread of Buddhism in the Uruvilva region.

The scriptures contain highly dramatic accounts of the confrontation between Shakyamuni and the three Kashyapa brothers. We are told that Shakyamuni, who was determined to convert Uruvilva Kashyapa, the eldest and most influential of the brothers, called upon him at his home, earnestly requesting that he be allowed to spend the night in the Hall of the Sacred Fire, which was monitored by the Kashyapas. Shakyamuni was warned that the hall was inhabited by an evil serpent that would surely do him harm, but he persisted in his request and was finally given permission. True to the warnings he had received, an evil serpent did in fact appear and attempt to attack Shakyamuni, who displayed such all-embracing mercy and compassion toward the serpent that he succeeded in subduing it.

The following morning, when Uruvilva Kashyapa learned what had happened, he was greatly impressed by Shakyamuni's powers. At the same time he remained convinced that his own abilities and accomplishments were superior. Then Shakyamuni performed other miracles and displays of mystical power until he eventually persuaded the Brahman master to acknowledge defeat.

There is, of course, some question as to just how literally we are to interpret such references to mystical powers and the like. In essence, the episode is probably intended to convey that Shakyamuni won an admission of defeat from his rival not through any superiority in philosophical debate but through his actual power and forcefulness as a man of religion.

In any event, Uruvilva Kashyapa, acknowledging complete submission before Shakyamuni, begged to become a disciple on the spot. Shakyamuni, we are told, admonished Uruvilva Kashyapa that, as the leader of a band of five hundred disciples of his own, he ought not to decide a matter of this importance in such haste. The Brahman master thereupon consulted with his disciples, and in the end he and his entire group of five hundred became followers of the Buddha, cutting off their hair braids and casting them into the river along with the vessels and implements used in their sacrificial rites. Moreover, his younger brothers, Nadi Kashyapa and Gaya Kashyapa, decided to follow his example. They and their bands of disciples likewise joined the Buddhist faith. Thus an entire Brahman sect, which had wielded such a powerful religious influence in the Uruvilva district and numbered some one thousand adherents in all, became a part of Shakyamuni's Order.

Such a mass conversion, hardly imaginable today, attests to both the skill and the effectiveness of Shakyamuni's preaching and practice and to the immense seriousness with which the ancient Indians viewed such religious and philosophical confrontations and their eagerness to place themselves under the guidance of whichever leader emerged victorious. Finally, it represents an important milestone in the history of the Order, for with it Shakyamuni's group of followers grew at one stroke into a religious body of substantial size. At the same time, it greatly facilitated the subsequent propagation of Buddhism in the kingdom of Magadha, where large numbers of people converted to Buddhism because of the veneration in which they held the Kashyapa brothers.

Perhaps the most eminent among Shakyamuni's converts in Magadha at this time was King Bimbisara, the ruler of the kingdom. We recall how the king had gone out to the foothills to meet Shakyamuni when the latter first passed through Magadha and how, realizing that Shakyamuni could not be moved by offers of worldly power or wealth, he had asked the young man to promise that when he found the enlightenment he was seeking, he would come at once and reveal it to the king.

The second meeting between Shakyamuni and the king seems to have taken place after the conversion of the Kashyapa brothers. Legend tells us that King Bimbisara, hearing that Shakyamuni had entered Rajagriha leading his new band of a thousand converts, hastened at once with his ministers and attendants to greet him. The king had no doubt heard rumors that Shakyamuni had attained Buddhahood and was overjoyed that the Enlightened One had not forgotten his earlier promise. Upon their meeting, the king received instruction in person from Shakyamuni and was converted to the faith.

King Bimbisara then donated an area of land known as the Bamboo Grove to Shakyamuni and his thousand disciples to serve as a temple or monastery to house them. At this early period, of course, there was nothing like the kind of formal arrangement of buildings that later came to be characteristic of Buddhist temples. The Bamboo Grove Monastery, which was situated outside the northern gate of the city, was probably nothing more than a simple shelter designed to protect the monks from the wind and rain.

In any event, Shakyamuni and his disciples spent most of their time begging alms or touring the countryside, and the monastery was therefore used only for rest and meditation during the rainy season. But though the Bamboo Grove Monastery may have been a modest establishment, its existence and the conversion of King Bimbisara that had brought about its establishment were important milestones in the gradual growth of the Buddhist Order, more far-reaching in their effect, perhaps, even than the mass conversion of the venerable Kashyapa brothers and their Brahman followers.

THE COMPANY
OF DISCIPLES

6

SHARIPUTRA AND MAUDGALYAYANA

In addition to King Bimbisara, there were many other important disciples and believers converted in Magadha who were later to exert a decisive influence upon the Buddhist Order. Most notable among them were Shariputra, Maudgalyayana, and Mahakashyapa, three of Shakyamuni's ten major disciples. All were converted while Shakyamuni was preaching the Law in Magadha.

Let us take up first the story of Shariputra and Maudgalyayana. Born of Brahman families in Magadha, they were close friends from childhood and enjoyed a wide reputation as young men of great talent and earnest students of the Brahmanic tradition. Dissatisfied with their formal Brahmanic studies, however, and hoping to find some higher truth, they began searching for a teacher. It was at this point that they heard of Sanjaya Belatthiputta, one of the six non-Buddhist teachers active in Magadha.

Sanjaya, it will be recalled, was noted for his nihilism and skepticism, questioning or even flatly rejecting many of the fundamental principles of Brahmanism. Shariputra and Maudgalyayana joined the band of some 250 disciples studying under Sanjaya and, as friendly rivals, diligently applied themselves to the task of mastering his teachings. Before long, they had become Sanjaya's chief disciples, and it is said that he even came to regard them as his successors. But in time they began to feel dissatisfied with their master's skeptical and nihil-istic philosophy, and they set about searching here and there for some more positive and compelling truth. At this time, they made a promise that whichever should first discover such a truth would not fail to let the other know. As it turned out, it was Shariputra who first had that good fortune.

In his fervent quest for a higher truth, Shariputra came into contact with Buddhism, though not through a direct meeting with Shakya-muni. His initial encounter was with Ashvajit, a disciple of Shakya-muni who was at the time begging alms in Rajagriha. Ashvajit is said to have been one of the five *bhikkhus*, or ascetics, to whom Shakyamuni addressed his first sermon. Early scriptural accounts say that Sharipu-tra was so impressed by Ashvajit's noble mien and air of self-possession that he asked him who his teacher was and what doctrine he taught.

The encounter took place on the outskirts of Rajagriha, where Ash-vajit had stopped to rest from his begging activities, and the answer he gave to Shariputra is of special importance. He replied that his teacher was Shakyamuni but added modestly that, since he himself had only recently entered the Buddhist Order, he was unable to give an adequate exposition of his teacher's doctrines.

Shariputra answered that even a partial explanation would be suffi-cient and once more begged Ashvajit to tell him something about his teacher's views. Ashvajit then complied by relating the portion of the Law that he understood in the following words:

> *All things spring from a cause.*
> *The Tathagata has explained the cause,*
> *And also how things cease to be.*

What Ashvajit was conveying in these words, of course, was the gist of Shakyamuni's first sermon, the law of cause and effect, of orig-ination and cessation. What seems striking about the incident is the extreme honesty and integrity displayed in Ashvajit's attitude. A man of lesser stature would surely have attempted to expound the Law to his questioner, even though his own grasp of it might be inadequate. But Ashvajit declined to speak at length out of reverence for the Buddha's teachings and for fear that he might in some way convey a misleading or erroneous impression of them. After all, the Law is not something that can be instantly grasped immediately upon entering the monastic order or the Buddhist community. As this episode indicates, one must spend much time in study and discipline to master it.

The second point to be noted in this episode is the fact that Shariputra, wise and perceptive as he was, was drawn to Ashvajit not by any eloquence or power of intellect displayed by the latter but by some indication of sanctity and deep religious faith that was apparent in his attitude and bearing. This, I believe, tells us something about the proper attitude to be adopted by those who are attempting to propagate the Law.

Ashvajit, though a novice, appears to have had a correct grasp of the theory of causation and the law of origination and cessation. A clear understanding of these and of the truth of life may be said to constitute the pillars of Buddhist philosophy. On hearing Ashvajit's exposition of the law of origination and cessation, we are told that Shariputra instantly comprehended the greatness of Shakyamuni's doctrine and realized that here at last was the truth for which he had been searching.

Shariputra was a young man of keen intelligence and philosophical insight, and he seems already to have had some inkling of the greatness of the Law when he first glimpsed Ashvajit. By listening to Ashvajit's rather brief exposition, his mind opened up and he attained a kind of understanding. In Buddhist terminology, he belonged to the category of voice-hearers (*shravaka*), those capable of gaining enlightenment simply by listening to an exposition of the principles of the Law. It is no wonder that, among Shakyamuni's principal disciples, he was to become known as "foremost in wisdom."

After his encounter with Ashvajit, Shariputra, true to the promise he and his friend had made, at once related to Maudgalyayana what had happened. Maudgalyayana, too, perceived the greatness of the Law, and he and Shariputra determined to become followers of Shakyamuni. But as the leading disciples of Sanjaya, they had been entrusted with the supervision of the 250 students under him, and it became necessary, therefore, for Shariputra and Maudgalyayana to discuss their momentous decision with the students. When they did so, we are told, all 250 asked to be allowed to join Shariputra and Maudgalyayana in becoming followers of the Buddha. Sanjaya, hearing what was afoot, did everything within his power to dissuade the two young men and block the move, but they held firm in their decision, as did the 250 students under them. Thus, in one stroke, Sanjaya was deprived of his entire following, and a whole sect, with the exception of its founder, converted to the Buddhist faith.

This was an event of tremendous import, for it meant the collapse of an entire school, one that had commanded considerable respect in the intellectual world of the time. It signaled the emergence of a new school of thought to take its place beside those of the six non-Buddhist teachers and opened the eyes of the people of the time to the advent of a powerful new religious philosophy to be reckoned with.

Scholars of Buddhist history attach great significance to the conversion of Shariputra and Maudgalyayana. In terms of intellectual history, it demonstrates that Buddhism was able to refute the skeptical and nihilistic trends of the time and gain acceptance among the populace. Buddhism is often mistaken as a religion of resignation or even nihilistic denial, but the conversion of Shariputra and Sanjaya's other followers demonstrates that the people of that time held no such attitude.

It is important to remember that disenchantment with Sanjaya's skepticism was what led Shariputra and Maudgalyayana to seek a higher truth elsewhere and in the end to embrace Buddhism. Their conversion is also of great significance because of the leading role that they later played in developing and systematizing the theoretical basis of the Buddhist Order.

Shakyamuni valued them highly, and there is much evidence of their outstanding contribution to the growth of the new religion. According to some accounts, when Shariputra and Maudgalyayana first came with their 250 students to ask for admission to the Buddhist Order, Shakyamuni predicted that these two men would become the foremost of all his disciples. Intuitively he seems to have sensed their outstanding qualities, and in fact placed such great expectation in them that other disciples were moved to jealousy.

Returning to the subject of Buddhism's refutation of nihilism, it is interesting to note how Shariputra acquired the enlightenment of a voice-hearer. According to the scriptural account, this came about when Shariputra and one of his fellow Brahmans was listening to Shakyamuni's discourse on skepticism. The Brahman, being a skeptic, argued that since all truth is essentially relative, there can be no absolutely objective truth and therefore all thought and philosophy are purely subjective. Shakyamuni replied that this view was in itself contradictory because, in maintaining that all truth is subjective or relative, one is already positing an absolute standard of judgment.

In this clear and compelling fashion, Shakyamuni not only refuted the assertions of the skeptics who were in vogue at the time but also conveyed an important hint as to the essential approach of Buddhism regarding such questions.

At this point, Shariputra, who was listening to this discourse as a bystander, gained enlightenment, and the Brahman skeptic, as one might expect, was converted.

When a new system of thought arises, it is natural that it not only expound its own ideas but attempt to refute the older or more popular doctrines of the time, and this is what we see Shakyamuni doing here. That he engaged in a veritable war of ideas is evidenced by the fact that many of his converts, such as the Kashyapa brothers, Shariputra, and Maudgalyayana, were among the leading intellectuals of the day.

It was to be expected that Shakyamuni would be counterattacked by his opponents. Pointing to the fact that influential Brahmans and promising young men of Rajagriha and other cities were converting to Buddhism in growing numbers, there were increasing accusations that Shakyamuni was "depriving parents of their sons and wives of their husbands, and bringing about the destruction of the family."

"All the young men of good family in Magadha have joined the Buddhist Order!" people exclaimed in alarm and asked who would be Shakyamuni's next objective, since he had already succeeded in luring away the disciples of the great Sanjaya.

No doubt the rapidity with which Buddhism swept through Magadha occasioned genuine alarm among the ordinary people, especially those closely allied with the older religions, who saw it as a menace to the conventional ways of society and even to the institution of the family. Needless to say, Buddhism represented no such sinister menace to society. Indeed, it does call for a fundamental spiritual reform, but at the same time it aims at building a better society and more enduring family solidarity. But to many people of Shakyamuni's time, who were content to judge merely by outward appearances, it seemed that his recruiting of disciples posed a serious threat to family life and other important social institutions, and he was accordingly attacked and maligned.

Shakyamuni is said to have brushed aside such criticisms as a temporary phenomenon and paid them little heed. And, just as he had predicted, the accusations against Buddhism eventually died down and he came to be revered as a truly great religious leader. But this process was to take many years. The true Law is always subject to a certain amount of blind opposition and slander. In preaching the Law, Shakyamuni was honored and revered by many during his lifetime as the Awakened One, but he was criticized and attacked by many as well. His so-called nine great ordeals, of which we shall have more to say later, were caused, if only indirectly, by the enmity and jealousy of his critics. During his forty-five years or more of ministry, he was often misunderstood and treated with prejudice by those around him. In spite of such hindrances and misunderstandings, however, he persisted in his efforts and, in the end, succeeded in elevating Buddhism to the level of a universal religion.

MAHAKASHYAPA

Also celebrated among Shakyamuni's ten principal disciples was Mahakashyapa, who was renowned as an austere and relentless seeker of the Way. Among Shakyamuni's followers he was known as the "foremost in the ascetic practices." It may be noted that, although Shakyamuni rejected as useless the severe ascetic practices advocated by many of the religious men of his time, he condoned the practice of *dhuta*, or mild ascetic precepts, such as limitations in food and clothing and living on alms, and it was these that Mahakashyapa was especially diligent in observing. After Shakyamuni's death, he presided over the First Buddhist Council and supervised the establishment of the Buddhist canon, thus playing a role of prime importance in the early Order. Before meeting Shakyamuni, he appears to have been, like so many of the Buddha's early disciples, a follower of Brahmanism. It is generally assumed that he was converted during the Magadha phase of Shakyamuni's ministry, although the exact time is not known. He came to be called Mahakashyapa after he joined the Buddhist Order. The honorific prefix *maha*, meaning "great," was added to his name to distinguish him from the three Kashyapa brothers from Uruvilva.

There are a great many anecdotes recorded concerning Mahakashyapa, most of them having to do with his austerity and sternness. He was held in awe within the Order for his extreme severity, but he was also criticized by some. According to one account, when he attained the stage of arhat, or one who has attained the highest of the four stages that voice-hearers aim to achieve, he presented his robe to Shakyamuni as a gesture of gratitude and received Shakyamuni's old robe in exchange. Mahakashyapa then proceeded to wear Shakyamuni's already well-worn robe until it was reduced to rags. This incident, and others like it, indicate that he was a man of great sincerity and integrity, but it is not difficult to understand why some of the other monks, failing to appreciate why he dressed in a ragged garment, treated him with disdain.

Another episode concerns the impeccable manner in which Mahakashyapa practiced the begging of alms. Alms begging had a twofold purpose. On one hand, it provided daily sustenance for the members of the Order; and on the other, it offered an opportunity for the laity to acquire religious merit and to establish a connection with the Buddha through their offerings.

The ethical principles governing almsgiving decreed that the members of the Order must eat any and all food offered to them by others without any sign of discrimination. Nevertheless, being human beings, the mendicants often found the food presented to them by the poor and humble to be somewhat less than appetizing. This is hardly surprising when one considers that many of the monks were young men who came from well-to-do families. As a result, it is said, they tended to walk rather slowly in front of the houses of the rich, drawing attention to their presence, but then trotted briskly past the houses of the poor.

Mahakashyapa, however, was an exception, upholding both the spirit and the letter of the Buddha's teachings and begging in a dignified manner that showed no trace of partiality to either rich or poor. People of sternness and integrity like Mahakashyapa, when their true motives are understood, are customarily treated with appropriate respect. But when their motives are not fully comprehended, they are often subject to misunderstanding and jealousy, and Mahakashyapa was no exception.

Another reason for the coldness or even antagonism that Mahakashyapa faced from some quarters would seem to be the fact that he was not skilled as a propounder of the Law. While men like Shariputra and Maudgalyayana distinguished themselves as brilliant theoreticians of the new religious organization, Mahakashyapa was distinguished mainly for the intensity and devotion with which he heeded Shakyamuni's teachings and put them into practice. For this reason, he did not enjoy great popularity. At the same time, he was indispensable to the Order in matters of administration, superintendence, and formulation of practice. Thus, it is certainly no accident that he played a central role in running the Order after Shakyamuni's death.

Shakyamuni himself seems to have valued Mahakashyapa extremely highly, though he was aware of the criticism, jealousy, and even hatred that Mahakashyapa provoked among some of the other disciples. Legend says that on one occasion Shakyamuni called his disciples together to defend Mahakashyapa from the mounting criticisms that were being voiced against him, and at that time, in order to show his high estimation of Mahakashyapa, he had him share his own seat. According to the accounts, Mahakashyapa is the only man who was ever accorded the honor of sharing the Buddha's seat. This incident shows the great confidence that Shakyamuni placed in him and his concern that Mahakashyapa be allowed to develop his good qualities without carping and interference from others.

Shakyamuni saw into the diverse characters of his disciples, particularly the so-called ten major disciples, and, as he guided and educated them toward the propagation of the Law, he allowed each one full scope for his abilities and talents. We can perceive from this how great was his understanding of people and his ability as a leader.

The anecdotes concerning Mahakashyapa also illustrate an important point in Buddhism, the fact that it does not seek to create a fixed image of the ideal person or demand that everyone conform to one particular stereotype. Rather, it encourages its adherents, while embracing a certain basic sense of mission, to give full play to their individual abilities and characteristics.

In addition to Mahakashyapa and the other major disciples, a great many converts to Buddhism were made in Magadha, including village headmen, heads of families, sons of wealthy commoners, and women. In embracing the new religion, these people were probably influenced by the example of King Bimbisara, the Kashyapa brothers, and the disciples of Sanjaya.

The teachings of Shakyamuni undoubtedly caused a considerable stir in Magadha, awakening the kingdom to a new sense of spiritual excitement and wonder. We have noted earlier the second meeting that took place between King Bimbisara and Shakyamuni when the latter, now a Buddha and accompanied by the Kashyapa brothers, reentered the city of Rajagriha. We are told that the king's ministers and court nobles assumed that Shakyamuni was a disciple of the prestigious Kashyapa brothers and were astounded when they learned that the situation was, in fact, the other way around. Shakyamuni's advent must have made a powerful impression upon the people of Magadha, convincing them that a new religion was on the rise, one that in time would supersede the religions of the past. It was this atmosphere of expectation and change that aided the propagation of the faith and facilitated the general acceptance of Buddhism by the people of the kingdom.

~

SUDATTA

The disciples and lay converts who embraced Shakyamuni's teachings during his lifetime came from all sectors and classes of Indian society. Within the Buddhist Order, they were treated without discrimination regardless of their position in secular society. Certain castes or class groups, however, seem to have played a particularly important role in spreading the Buddhist teachings, notably the members of the Kshatriya, or warrior class, and the rich merchants. The merchants, who were rising to prominence in society, seem to have been particularly attracted to the new religion. Discontented with the rigidity of the old social order, they longed for greater freedom of movement and the opportunity to exercise their initiative in personal and social affairs. It was for this reason that they welcomed Buddhism, so different in its liberality and pliancy from the rigid conventionalism of Brahmanism, and made it the spiritual support of their lives.

Buddhism, it should be noted, not only condones business activities on the part of its lay adherents but positively stresses the importance of such activities. Those believers who left family life and became monks, of course, renounced all such activities and lived the life of wandering mendicants, but those who remained in lay society were encouraged to practice industry and frugality and see to the support of their families and relatives. Buddhism takes the view that although the fundamental truths of the religion exist on a wholly different plane from daily social and commercial activities, the former are indispensable for the well being of people engaged in such activities. From the perspective of Buddhism, religion should not attempt to dictate social activity but should exert a spiritual influence over those who carry out that activity. Buddhism did in fact exercise a strong influence among one particularly active group in society, the wealthy merchants, who in this time of rapid social change were coming increasingly to the fore.

The most famous of these merchant followers of Buddhism was Sudatta. He was a resident of Shravasti in Kosala, the powerful state that lay northwest of and dominated Shakyamuni's native state. It was in the city of Rajagriha in Magadha, however, that his conversion took place.

Sudatta was visiting Rajagriha, perhaps on a business trip, and was staying at the home of a wealthy merchant who had already converted to Buddhism and had apparently invited Shakyamuni and his followers to his home the following day. Sudatta, observing the bustle of preparation that was going on among his friend's family and servants, inquired what guests he was expecting, whereupon the merchant replied, "Tomorrow morning a Buddha is coming."

On hearing the word *Buddha*, Sudatta was filled with astonishment. Though famed for his great wealth, Sudatta was also well known as a generous dispenser of charity, having acquired the name Anathapindada, or "Supplier of the Needy," because of his donations to the poor. Clearly a religious man, he could hardly have failed to be astounded at the news that a Buddha, or Enlightened One, the ideal figure in Indian religious thought, was to appear the next morning at the very house where he was staying. Deeply stirred, he waited impatiently for the night to pass. When dawn came, he slipped out of the house early and made his way to the grove where Shakyamuni was seated in meditation. Shakyamuni is said to have preached to him, and he thereupon determined to become a follower of the new religion.

Sudatta's conversion is of considerable significance, for it is believed to have paved the way for the propagation of the Law in the state of Kosala. Later he donated a park and monastery in Shravasti to the Buddhist Order. Built on land that he purchased from Prince Jeta, the heir to the ruler of Kosala, it was known as the Jetavana *vihara*, or monastery. The name is well known in Japanese literature because of the famous opening passage of the *Tale of the Heike*, which speaks of the bells of that monastery tolling the impermanence of life. I suppose it would be pedantic to point out that, according to some scholars, bells were not used in Buddhist monasteries in Shakyamuni's time.

～

Shakyamuni's Visit to Kapilavastu

The conversion of Sudatta, the wealthiest man in Kosala, must have caused some stir among the other states, particularly Shakyamuni's native kingdom of Kapilavastu, which was politically dependent upon Kosala.

Shakyamuni is said to have returned home for the first time after completing his preaching of the Law in the state of Magadha. But as is so often the case with the events of his life, different sources give very different dates for the visit, one placing it two years after his enlightenment, others six years or even twelve years after. All we can say for certain is that he returned home only after he had spent some time preaching in Magadha, had seen the Law widely accepted there, and had firmly established the foundations of his new religious order.

This was not the only time Shakyamuni visited Kapilavastu, of course. During the forty-five or fifty years of his ministry, he must have gone there a number of times, especially in view of the fact that he carried on preaching activities in the neighboring state of Kosala. These subsequent visits, however, could not have had the deep meaning and emotional impact, either for him or for the members of his family, that his first return must have had. He was returning home to face his father and kinsmen not as an ordinary man but as a Buddha, an Enlightened One.

Apparently the news of his attainment of Buddhahood reached Kapilavastu ahead of him. But the Shakyas were by nature a rather proud and unbending people, conservative in their religious views and inclined to hold fast to the conventions of Brahmanism and the local cults of the region. Though Shakyamuni's family and tribesmen welcomed with warmth and courtesy this man who had once been the prince and heir of their kingdom, they do not seem to have been very responsive to the doctrines he taught. According to scriptural accounts, it was only after he had demonstrated various mystical powers that his relatives were inclined to listen seriously to what he was saying. Then he set about preaching the Law to them one by one and in the end succeeded in making a number of converts.

First to be converted was Shakyamuni's father, King Shuddhodana, along with Shakyamuni's son, Rahula, and his younger half-brother,

Nanda. In subsequent visits to the state, Shakyamuni gained other prominent disciples, such as Upali, Aniruddha, Ananda, and Devadatta, of whom we shall speak later. Rahula was still in his teens at the time of his conversion; later he became a prominent disciple and was highly praised as foremost among those who love to practice self-discipline. Since he had been a mere infant when Shakyamuni renounced family life and set out from Kapilavastu, he could not have had any recollection of his father. It was Princess Yashodhara, we are told, who arranged for him to meet his father, though she herself declined to have an interview with her former husband. Shakyamuni entrusted his son to the care of Shariputra, who was accompanying him on his visit home, and Rahula was made a novice in the Order. Later, he joined his father in the preaching of the Law and played a very active role in the propagation of the new faith.

A third member of Shakyamuni's immediate family, his younger half-brother, Nanda, was also converted on the occasion of this first visit to Kapilavastu. After Shakyamuni renounced secular life and left the kingdom, Nanda had taken his place as heir to King Shuddhodana, and he was just about to be married to the beautiful Princess Sundari when Shakyamuni reappeared in Kapilavastu to preach the Law. The circumstances under which he was persuaded to renounce his claim to the throne, call off his forthcoming marriage, and enter the Buddhist Order are not fully known, though one cannot help feeling a little sorry for the young man, considering the abrupt way in which his life was disrupted by his older brother's appearance.

It is said that after becoming a monk, he was unable to banish thoughts of the secular world from his mind and was tormented by doubt, which suggests that perhaps the decision to enter the Order had not been made entirely of his own free will. With the help of Shakyamuni's careful guidance and instruction, however, he eventually freed himself from worldly desires and devoted his full energies to the practice of the Way.

~

ANANDA

In time, a number of members of the Shakya tribe became followers and ardent supporters of Shakyamuni. Ananda, Aniruddha, and
Devadatta were converted to the Order sometime after Shakyamuni's
first visit to his home state. All three were cousins of Shakyamuni, and
Ananda and Devadatta were brothers. It would seem that practically
all the younger members of the Shakya tribe became Buddhists. Most
prominent among these three was Ananda, who became Shakyamuni's
favorite disciple and constant attendant for the last twenty-five years of
his life. Described as "foremost in the protection of the Law," Ananda
was gifted with perfect recall, which allowed him to recite from memory the sermons and pronouncements of the Buddha.

It is not known just when Ananda was converted, but because of
his relative youthfulness, it could hardly have taken place on Shakyamuni's first visit to Kapilavastu. Most likely it occurred some twenty
years after Shakyamuni's enlightenment. Ananda was in his twenties
at the time. Since he was among the most important disciples, there
are many anecdotes concerning him. Along with Mahakashyapa, he
played a central role in the activities of the Order after the Buddha's
entry into nirvana and is especially famous for having recited all the
sutras from memory at the First Buddhist Council.

The peculiar thing about this event is that Ananda was at first
excluded from the Council on the grounds that he alone, among all
the five hundred disciples of the Buddha who had gathered to put
their leader's teachings in order, had not attained the state of arhat.
Ananda, greatly distressed, gave himself up to intense meditation and,
we are told, became an arhat on the morning of the day that the Council was to begin its work, after which he was duly admitted to it by
Mahakashyapa.

This anecdote indicates that Ananda was treated rather distantly and even coldly by the older and more seasoned members of the Order. We are also told that the fastidious Mahakashyapa was critical of Ananda's conduct, complaining that in his role as Shakyamuni's personal attendant he failed to display the proper reverence toward the Buddha. Mahakashyapa also condemned him for his part in allowing women to be admitted to the Order. There may, of course, have been aspects of Ananda's personality and behavior that justified such criticisms. I am inclined to believe, however, that at least some of the animosity displayed toward Ananda by the older members of the Order was motivated by the fact that he was Devadatta's brother.

Devadatta, as we shall see, caused enormous trouble to Shakyamuni and to the Order as a whole, eventually going so far as to make an attempt on the Buddha's life. Perhaps it is only natural that the other members of the Order, in spite of the promptings of their better nature, should have ill feelings toward Ananda. Another factor that may have contributed to the general feeling of mistrust was the jealousy that he aroused because of his closeness to the Buddha.

One must also consider Ananda's attitude toward women. He is often portrayed in the scriptures as questioning Shakyamuni about women, and it was through his repeated pleas that women were finally admitted to the Order and the category of *bhikkhuni*, or Buddhist nun, was created. This, needless to say, made Ananda very popular with the nuns, if that is not too frivolous a way to express it, but it may not have sat well with the older male members of the Order.

In any event, whatever feelings of envy, disapproval, or sheer awe Ananda may have aroused among his fellow monks, he remained constantly at Shakyamuni's side as his favorite disciple. If his attitude toward women and the charges leveled by Mahakashyapa against him indicate a certain unconventionality and lack of restraint in his makeup, he was at the same time, I am certain, a warm and mild-natured person. Otherwise, he could hardly have played the part of personal attendant to Shakyamuni for some twenty-five years. Shakyamuni had had other attendants before Ananda but had not retained any of them for more than a short time. There is no doubt that of all his attendants, Ananda was the one to whom he felt closest.

UPALI AND ANIRUDDHA

The other notable disciples from the kingdom of the Shakyas were Upali and Aniruddha, both of whom are counted among the ten major disciples of the Buddha. Upali was praised as "foremost in observing the precepts" (*vinaya*), while Aniruddha was "foremost in divine insight."

Upali was unique among the ten major disciples in one particular way. Whereas the others had all been students of Brahmanism or were members of the Shakya royal family, Upali came from a much more humble background and social station, having originally been a barber at the court of Kapilavastu.

Shakyamuni, we are told, thought highly of Upali and treated him with great respect, a point, it seems to me, that is important to note. Hiromoto Mizuno, along with other Buddhist scholars, has suggested that Shakyamuni deliberately adopted a respectful and even protective attitude toward Upali in an effort to combat the deep-rooted prejudices against the common people that were prevalent among the Shakya clan and other members of the upper classes. Shakyamuni wished to demonstrate that Buddhism is fundamentally egalitarian in its attitude and that within the Buddhist Order, conventional class and caste distinctions have no validity.

The only differences of rank among the disciples were those based upon the length of time a person had belonged to the Order. Monks who had received ordination early in Shakyamuni's preaching career took precedence over those who had entered the Order later. Among Upali and the three young nobles of the Shakya family, Aniruddha, Ananda, and Devadatta, who were converted as a group, Upali was the first one to receive ordination, hence he was considered the senior among them, followed by Aniruddha and Ananda in that order. This indicates that Shakyamuni took scrupulous care to see that the fundamental Buddhist principle of equality was reflected in the functioning of the Order. And, as though in response to such thoughtful treatment, Upali did his best to live up to Shakyamuni's expectations, in time becoming an outstanding member of the Order and distinguishing himself for the unparalleled zeal with which he observed the rules of discipline.

Along with Upali, Aniruddha is a figure of considerable interest. He was pronounced "foremost in divine insight" because, although blind, he is said to have had extraordinary powers of discernment. There is an interesting if somewhat curious account of how he came to be blind. A cousin of Shakyamuni, he had entered the Order full of ardor and determination. One day, while listening to the Buddha's preaching of the Law, he dozed off and, as a result, was severely scolded by Shakyamuni. He thereupon determined that he would never commit the same offense again. We do not know exactly what method he employed to ensure that he would never fall asleep, but it must have been rather drastic, and Aniruddha carried it out with such unflagging resolution that eventually he went blind. I am not certain how far we should go in accepting the credibility of such a story. If it is true, however, it certainly indicates that in matters pertaining to the Law, Aniruddha was a man of inflexible determination.

The other disciples who were members of the Shakya family were Shakyamuni's aunt Mahaprajapati, the first nun to be admitted to the Order, and his cousin Devadatta, who later turned against him and about whom we will have much to say in the chapters that follow.

THE GROWTH OF
THE ORDER

7

THE OTHER MAJOR DISCIPLES

We have already discussed most of the so-called ten major disciples of Shakyamuni, but there remain three about whom something should be said: Purna, Katyayana, and Subhuti.

Purna was praised as being "foremost in preaching the Law." Unrivaled in the eloquence with which he could expound the doctrine, he came from a rather different background from most of Shakyamuni's other major disciples. Neither a Brahman nor a son of the aristocracy, he belonged, like Sudatta, to the class of wealthy merchants and is said to have amassed a huge fortune through commerce and trade.

Purna was not a native of central India, where Shakyamuni's preaching activities were concentrated, but came from a seaport town in western India that was situated north of the modern city of Mumbai and hence was far removed from the circle of Buddhist influence of the time.

One may wonder how a man engaged in commercial enterprise and living in an area so remote from Buddhist activity could possibly have become a disciple of Shakyamuni. It came about, we are told, in the following way. Purna was apparently well known among merchants and traders, and his fame had reached even as far as Shravasti, the capital of Kosala. A group of Shravasti merchants, having heard of his reputation, appeared at his home on the seacoast and asked if he would join them in a commercial voyage, thinking no doubt that with the benefit of Purna's experience they could turn a large profit. Purna readily consented and the party set out.

As it happened, the Shravasti merchants were all lay converts to Buddhism, and during the voyage they regularly gathered in a group to perform their devotions. We do not know exactly what form such devotions took at that time, though presumably they involved some sort of repeated recitation of Shakyamuni's teachings. Purna, his curiosity aroused, asked what they were doing, and they told him about Shakyamuni and his teachings. Purna was deeply moved and, when the voyage was over, immediately set off for Shravasti, where he heard the Buddha preach and determined to become a member of the Order.

One cannot help wondering whether Purna's rather unusual background had something to do with his widely recognized skill in preaching the Law. His long and at times no doubt trying experiences as a merchant had probably taught him a great deal about human nature, and, like any good businessman, he had learned to read the minds of the people with whom he dealt. In later years, when he turned to the preaching of the Law, he utilized these abilities, skillfully adjusting his delivery to the capacity of his audience and presenting the teachings of Buddhism in such a fashion that they would make the greatest possible impression upon his listeners. He was a forceful leader, who, having grown up with the common people and made his living among them, knew well how to reach them with the Buddha's message.

Katyayana, also known as Mahakatyayana, was a native of Ujjayini, the capital of the state of Avanti. A Brahman by birth, he held a position as religious adviser and confidential secretary to the ruler of that state. Though there is no indication that Shakyamuni himself ever visited Avanti, situated in the western part of central India, it is mentioned frequently in the sutras and other Buddhist writings, probably as a result of Katyayana's activities. He was the first native of Avanti to become a disciple of the Buddha and was considered "foremost in debate."

Like Purna, he was converted at Shravasti, where he had been sent by the ruler of Avanti, who had heard reports of Shakyamuni's teachings. At the Jetavana Monastery, he had occasion to listen to Shakyamuni preaching the Law and was so moved that he instantly determined to become a member of the Order. Shakyamuni then sent him back to Avanti, where he succeeded in converting the king and many others to the new faith. He seems to have been a skilled theoretician who was especially adept at categorizing and systematizing the various pronouncements of the Buddha and presenting them in lucid and trenchant form.

The last of the great disciples to be discussed, Subhuti, seems by comparison with the other members of the group to be singularly lacking in color and individuality. It might fairly be said that he is characterized principally by his lack of characteristics. There are almost no anecdotes connected with his name, and one is puzzled to understand how he happened to be numbered among the ten major disciples. In later centuries he was regarded as having been "foremost in understanding the doctrine of non-substantiality" (*shunyata*), though I wonder if this is accurate. In the Wisdom sutras, which deal with this doctrine, he is addressed by the Buddha as the one who has grasped the doctrine of non-substantiality most clearly. And yet, in contrast with men like Shariputra and Maudgalyayana, he was hardly a conspicuous figure in the Order, which one would guess he should have been if he was really "foremost in understanding the doctrine of non-substantiality."

To explain this apparent discrepancy, the well-known Buddhist scholar Fumio Masutani suggests that Subhuti was distinguished not for any profound understanding of metaphysical doctrine but rather for his balanced and well-rounded personality. He was a nephew of Sudatta, the wealthy philanthropist who donated the Jetavana Monastery to Shakyamuni and his followers, but in spite of this connection, his role in the activities of the Order appears to have been an unassuming one. Perhaps, surrounded by men of greater intellectual brilliance and force of character, the tolerant and mild-mannered Subhuti served as a kind of shock absorber within the Order. Shakyamuni may deliberately have held up this gentle and modest man as a model for the other members of the Order, hoping that his example would have a beneficial influence.

Although we have only legends and scattered anecdotes upon which to base a judgment, when examining the accounts pertaining to these ten great disciples of Shakyamuni, we cannot help being struck by the disparate nature of their personalities, the diversity of their talents and resources, and the remarkable way in which Shakyamuni succeeded in making use of these.

People tend naturally to gravitate toward those whose personalities please them or who possess abilities and traits similar to their own. But no one who even unconsciously reveals such partiality can be called a leader in the true sense. The true leader is one who can skillfully draw out and develop the potential of all types of people, even those who differ radically from or are uncongenial to oneself, and utilize them in creating a well-balanced and harmonious whole. Shakyamuni was an outstanding example of such a leader, principally, I would suggest, because his method of developing the varied resources of the people under him was based on an overall understanding of human nature in all its manifold aspects.

THE CITY OF SHRAVASTI

Purna, Katyayana, and Subhuti were all converted by Shakyamuni in the city of Shravasti, though only Subhuti was a native of the city, the other two having come from far away to listen to Shakyamuni's sermons. This suggests the important role that the city itself played as a center of Buddhist activities.

Chinese translations of the scriptures speak of "the three hundred thousand of Shravasti," though whether this is to be taken as an accurate count of the population of Kosala's capital is a matter of debate. It is said that one-third of Shravasti's population attended Shakyamuni's sermons, one-third heard his teachings though they never saw him, and one-third neither saw nor heard of him. This suggests that well over half the population of the city was either converted to or favorably disposed toward Buddhism, and this supposition is borne out by other sources. From this, we can surmise the great impact that the work of the Buddhist Order must have had upon the city.

Why, one may ask, was Buddhism so widely known and accepted in Shravasti? Shakyamuni and his followers at first centered their activities on the city of Rajagriha in Magadha, and only extended them to Shravasti, some distance to the north, at a much later period. According to one theory, the rapid growth of Buddhism in Shravasti was initially due in large part to the efforts of the rich merchant Sudatta, who returned to the city after having been converted in Rajagriha. As the first Buddhist believer in the city, he laid the foundation upon which the faith would later flourish and spread. We have seen, for example, that he bought a plot of land from the crown prince of the state and constructed the Jetavana Monastery, providing a place where the members of the Order could spend the rainy season.

There is a clear demarcation between the dry season and the rainy season in India, and it is common practice to calculate time in terms of so many rainy seasons rather than so many years. After Sudatta had built the Jetavana Monastery for them, Shakyamuni and his followers customarily spent the rainy season there, studying and meditating. In later years, this monsoon retreat in Shravasti became a headquarters for Shakyamuni's preaching activities. But, as the sources attest, there were to be many frustrations and setbacks before Buddhism could become the dominant religion in Shravasti. Shakyamuni encountered numerous attacks and persecutions during his lifetime, the best known being the so-called nine great ordeals. These include a the treacherous plot on the part of Devadatta as well as hostile acts directed at the Order during its early days in Shravasti.

Various reasons have been suggested as to why Shakyamuni was subjected to such persecutions, but there is no doubt that it had to do with the religious situation in Kosala at the time. Both Kosala and Magadha had suddenly risen to political prominence shortly before Shakyamuni's time. To their capitals came the leaders of new Brahmanic sects, such as the six non-Buddhist teachers who resided in Rajagriha, as well as various wandering ascetics. The religious scene was dominated by the ferment of their new ideas and theories. At the same time, traditional Brahmans continued to be highly respected at the courts of the rulers of these states, though their activities were conventionalized and pertained mainly to matters of ritual. Under such circumstances, it is not surprising that Shakyamuni met with opposition from these various groups in his efforts to propagate the Law.

Though Shakyamuni and his disciples had the Jetavana Monastery to use as a base for their activities, the atmosphere that surrounded them was by no means entirely friendly. On the contrary, the Brahmans resorted to all manner of devices to discredit Shakyamuni and his teachings. One plot involved a courtesan named Chincha, who pretended to be pregnant and claimed that Shakyamuni was the father.

In another incident, the Brahmans, after spreading rumors linking Shakyamuni with a courtesan named Sundari, had the woman killed and put out the rumor that her death was the work of the Buddhist monks. To such lengths were the Brahmans willing to go in an effort to maintain their power and position and to combat what they regarded as a threat to their status. However, Shakyamuni was able to endure and overcome such obstacles, conquering them through the power of truth and reason and opening the way for the spread of the Law.

Every revolution has its counterrevolution, and any new humanistic religion is bound to face almost inhuman attack from the established powers of society. The teachers of the new religion, however, must push ahead, confident in their future and prepared to persevere in the face of criticism and slander. The accounts of the Buddhist activities in Shravasti, where, eventually, a majority of the inhabitants were converted, show that its widespread propagation was due to the courageous efforts of Shakyamuni and his disciples.

The scriptures record another anecdote that illustrates the kind of opposition and animosity that the new religion faced from older religious groups. This concerns the confrontation between Shakyamuni and a Brahman living in Shravasti who worshipped the fire god Agni and was known to be extremely dogmatic in matters pertaining to caste. When he saw Shakyamuni begging for alms, he immediately called him a "base, lowly monk," as he was accustomed to do whenever he met any non-Brahman mendicant. Shakyamuni replied to his words of abuse by saying, "No Brahman is such by birth; no outcaste is such by birth. An outcaste is such by his deeds; a Brahman is such by his deeds."

This reply, I think, sums up very well the Buddhist attitude toward the caste and class system. "An outcaste is such by his deeds; a Brahman is such by his deeds" — in other words, a person's true worth is determined not by an accident of birth but by the kind of life that person leads. This statement demonstrates that a very pragmatic ethic, with a strikingly modern tone, was being preached some twenty-five hundred years ago. It also indicates clearly that, according to Buddhism, an individual's way of life takes precedence over any hierarchical distinctions that may be imposed by the social system of the time.

Some scholars, noting that Shakyamuni rejected the distinctions laid down by the caste system, ask why he did not go a step further and actively work to overthrow the system. They find it somehow condemnable that he was not more thoroughgoing in his repudiation of caste and class. But such criticisms fail to take into account the true nature of Shakyamuni's mission. He was not, after all, a social agitator or reformer but the founder of a new religion, whose chief concern was the spreading of the Law. He sought to look beyond the facade of social structure and organization to observe the basic ills that beset humankind and to devise some effective means by which to free people from their sufferings. With this end in view, he set forth a universal system of truths and ethical values, a system that transcended the society and age in which he lived.

The system, or perhaps one should say the way of life, that he taught denied the validity of the class and caste distinctions that prevailed in Indian society at that time, but this does not necessarily mean that Shakyamuni himself was obligated to carry out a program of social reform. He concentrated on defining the basic principles and premises according to which people should live and left it to his adherents to consider whether these principles could be reconciled with the existing social order or necessitated some kind of social reform.

Too often, it seems to me, we try to understand the individual strictly in terms of the society and period that produced him rather than the other way around. Thus, with Shakyamuni, we ask about his attitude toward the social institutions and ills of his time and, on the basis of the answers we arrive at, attempt to surmise what sort of person he was. In the case of Shakyamuni, and in a broader sense of all great religious leaders, such an approach is inappropriate. Shakyamuni and men like him are primarily concerned not with social institutions but with more basic problems of human existence and human worth. Only when we consider them in the light of their responses to these basic questions can we evaluate them correctly.

It is well to remember that Shakyamuni not only openly expressed his disapproval of the traditional distinctions of class and caste but also enforced a strictly egalitarian approach within the religious Order that he founded. As demonstrated earlier, he completely disregarded questions of race, caste, or class in the organization and daily functioning of the Buddhist Order. Regardless of whether a monk had been born as a Brahman, a Kshatriya, a Vaishya, or a Shudra, all members were on equal footing. Thus, although Shakyamuni did not attempt to carry out any sweeping social reform that would do away with the class and caste system entirely, he founded within the society of his time an organization that rejected all class and caste distinctions, certainly an act that can be viewed as a step in the direction of eventual social reform.

Returning to the subject of Buddhist activities in the city of Shravasti, we should note that, in addition to the Jetavana Monastery, there was another Buddhist establishment on the outskirts of the city. This was the Mrigara-matri Hall, which was situated to the east of the Jetavana Monastery. The hall was donated to the Order by a woman adherent of the faith named Vishakha. The daughter of a wealthy man of the state of Anga, she became a fervent believer in Buddhism at an early age. Later, she married a rich merchant of Shravasti. On the occasion of her wedding, the groom invited five hundred naked Brahman ascetics to help solemnize the proceedings, but she raised strong objections and had them sent away. She then began to tell the groom and his parents about the teachings of Shakyamuni and converted the entire family.

It must have been quite unheard of in those days for a bride marrying into a family whose religious faith differed from her own to speak out so boldly, and what is more, to succeed in winning over all her in-laws to her own persuasion. Evidently she was a woman of forceful character and certainly a model of the proselytizing spirit.

Her husband's family, whose surname was Mrigara, was profoundly impressed by her religious zeal and addressed her as *Matri*, or Mother, because of her seniority in the faith. Thus she came to be known as Mrigara-matri even among the ordinary citizens of Shravasti, by whom she was admired and respected.

In time, with the help of such zealous supporters as Sudatta and Mrigara-matri, the Buddhist Order overcame the opposition and hostility that it initially faced and spread its teachings among the citizens of Shravasti. An event that had great bearing upon this process, and which gives us much to think about even today, was the conversion of King Prasenajit, the ruler of Kosala. He seems to have been converted to Buddhism relatively early and became a devoted patron of the faith after observing the extraordinary respect and reverence with which Shakyamuni was treated by the common people of his state.

In ancient India, heads of state and Brahman priests were customarily accorded the highest degree of respect. And yet, as King Prasenajit observed with his own eyes, Shakyamuni was capable of inspiring within his followers a love and respect far transcending that paid to any worldly monarch. In the end, the king found himself moved to the same kind of reverence for the Buddha and his teachings. This is one more proof that the Law is capable of stirring people's innermost hearts in a way that mere wealth and temporal authority never can.

There are numerous other accounts of Shakyamuni's proselytizing activities in Shravasti, which is hardly surprising in view of the fact that so many of the inhabitants are said to have been won over to Buddhism. Among the most colorful tales is one that deals with the conversion of the notorious brigand Angulimala. In Chinese translations of the scriptures, he is often referred to as "Necklace of Fingers," a curious name and one that derives from the fact that he wore an ornamental necklace made of the severed fingers of people he had murdered.

A Brahman by birth and formerly a student of Brahmanic learning, he is said to have been tricked and betrayed by his teacher and his teacher's wife and thereafter to have turned to a life of evil, causing widespread terror among the people of the time. The scriptures give a highly dramatic account of how Shakyamuni, determined to save the young man, went out to meet him. The young man attempted to attack Shakyamuni, but the latter fended him off with various magical powers and in the end converted him.

The story of Angulimala is no doubt intended to illustrate that even the most evil and vicious of people can be saved through the great compassion of the Buddha. It also indicates that true religion does not merely bring solace to the spirit but is a vital, active force that does not hesitate to plunge into the midst of the dangers and sordidness of the world to rescue people of all types from suffering.

MANAGEMENT OF THE ORDER

With its main base of operations at the Jetavana Monastery in Shravasti, the Buddhist Order appears to have spread over a very wide area of India. Various sources indicate that, in addition to Shravasti and Rajagriha, Buddhism was well established in Shaketa, Varanasi, Vaishali, Kaushambi, and Ujjayini, all situated along the middle reaches of the Ganges River. From this it may be inferred that Shakyamuni and his disciples proselytized mainly in central India, teaching in towns and villages along the caravan routes.

In the cities mentioned above, the citizens lent their support to Buddhism, though not perhaps as enthusiastically as the inhabitants of Shravasti, and donated monasteries. These latter include the Saptaparna-guha, or Cave of the Seven Leaves, in Rajagriha, where the First Buddhist Council was later held; the Great Forest Monastery near Vaishali; and the Deer Park Monastery at Varanasi. From this we can surmise that these cities acted as centers for the propagation of Buddhism in central India.

As converts and itinerant monks increased in number and more centers of Buddhist activity opened, it became necessary to establish rules and precepts for the governing of the Order.

In his later years, Shakyamuni, while continuing to preach the Law, is said to have given much thought to the administrative problems involved in the running of the Buddhist Order. At first the Order consisted simply of a community of monks. Later the assembly of nuns was established and two more groups, those of male and female lay believers, were added. Thus the Order came to be made up of four assemblies: *bhikkhus* (monks), *bhikkhunis* (nuns), *upasakas* (laymen), and *upasikas* (laywomen).

It is not certain just what rules and precepts Shakyamuni devised for the running of the Order. Scriptural sources list 250 precepts for the monks and 500 precepts for the nuns, but these were apparently compiled at a later date. It is doubtful that such complicated rules of discipline existed during Shakyamuni's lifetime, although undoubtedly there were detailed rules for the ordination of monks and nuns and the other rituals of the Order.

We know, for instance, that all members of the Order were enjoined to pay the highest respect to the three treasures, namely the Buddha, the Law, and the Buddhist Order, while in religious practice emphasis was placed upon meditation and the cultivation of *prajna*, or wisdom, as well as on the keeping of the precepts.

For the lay believers, the five precepts were set forth. These commanded the believer to refrain from taking life, taking what is not given, committing adultery, telling lies, and drinking intoxicants. But these precepts appear to be more in the nature of ethical standards that the believers were expected to observe than a form of religious practice. The basic religious practice of the believer, we can surmise, was conceived to be the contemplation of the Law, the cultivation of wisdom, and the reform and improvement of the individual.

Judging from Shakyamuni's teachings and what we know of his manner of preaching, his approach seems to have been rather lenient and tolerant. It is therefore difficult to believe that he devised the 250 precepts for monks and 500 precepts for nuns that are found in the scriptures. These minute and sometimes rigorous rules were more probably drawn up after his entry into nirvana, perhaps because members of the Order felt that only in this way could proper discipline be maintained. Unfortunately, they have led some to the mistaken view that Buddhism is severe in its demands upon its followers. Shakyamuni himself appears to have been a man of very few wants and desires, but in preaching to others he did not force them to practice strict asceticism or denial of all desires. On the contrary, he taught his followers to lead a life of moderation, avoiding both hedonism and extreme self-denial. The Middle Way, as we have seen, is a basic doctrine of Buddhism, and though the monk or nun was undoubtedly expected to follow a more austere way of life than the lay believer, neither monk nor layman was expected to depart from this central ideal of moderation.

In the early days of Shakyamuni's preaching career, as we have mentioned above, no women were allowed in the Order. Though they requested admittance in increasing numbers, Shakyamuni is said to have refused their requests, and it was only in his later years that, through the efforts of Ananda, he was persuaded to change his mind. The first female member of the Order was Mahaprajapati, Shakyamuni's aunt, who from his infancy acted as a mother to him.

Given that throughout his life Shakyamuni taught the equality of all human beings and repudiated the conventional distinctions of caste and class, one wonders why he took such an apparently biased view of women and for so long excluded them from the Order. This is a difficult question and one that no doubt requires further study by scholars before it can be properly answered. My own feeling, however, is that he did not despise women or look down on them. Nowhere in his teachings do we find any general statement on women or any indication that they are to be classed apart from men.

It is interesting to note the pronouncements that Shakyamuni is recorded to have made concerning the duties of a husband and wife. He remarks that a wife should manage the household competently, treat her husband's friends and acquaintances with respect, take care of the property, and be chaste and diligent. But he also states that it is the duty of a husband to be courteous and faithful to his wife, to give her due authority in managing household affairs, and to buy her clothes and adornments.

Far from suggesting that Shakyamuni had any basic prejudice

against women, this would seem to be a very understanding and enlightened view of a woman's role in the marriage relationship, or at least one that would have seemed remarkably enlightened for the times. One should keep in mind that, in ancient India, the position of women was generally very low. Even in prosperous households, women were treated as little better than slaves once they had finished bearing children. And if they failed to produce any male heirs, their husbands could divorce them with ease. In a society that constantly emphasized the superiority of men over women, Shakyamuni's attitude was decidedly progressive.

Nevertheless, when it came to questions of the admittance and position of women in the Order, Shakyamuni's response was surprisingly strict. Perhaps he wanted to protect his disciples from distraction and make certain that there would be no disruption in the daily discipline and religious practice. He was anxious that his followers, once they had become monks, should reach the same high level of enlightenment that he himself had attained, but he knew that this required great effort and concentration. The monks had renounced secular life and set out upon the path toward higher understanding. For this reason, they had to be sheltered from any influence that might frustrate their efforts and deflect them from their course. It was with concerns of this kind, I believe, that Shakyamuni hesitated for so long to admit women to the Order.

In Buddhist literature, one frequently finds women alluded to as "animality incarnate" or "the cause of five obstacles," but such phrases, hyperbolic though they may be, are probably intended simply as a device to warn monks away from any unseemly involvement with women.

We know from the Indian literature of the time that women were customarily looked upon as lustful and quarrelsome by nature. Eventually, in the scriptures of the Mahayana schools of Buddhism, especially the Lotus Sutra, we find it clearly stated that women are capable of attaining Buddhahood. This doctrine, in my opinion, has its roots in the teachings of Shakyamuni himself, who stressed the equality of all human beings as the fundamental truth of his teachings. The fact that, at Ananda's urging, he welcomed women into the Order clearly attests to this.

DEVADATTA'S REVOLT

With the admission of Mahaprajapati, the Order came to consist of both monks and nuns, and the number of nuns increased considerably in Shakyamuni's later years. Among the most notable were Khema, the consort of King Bimbisara, who was regarded as "foremost in wisdom" among the nuns; Utpalavarna, the daughter of a Shravasti merchant; and Dammadina, who was regarded as "foremost in preaching."

In the course of the growth and development of the Order, a very serious event occurred. This was the revolt of Devadatta, which caused the Buddha considerable anxiety in his closing years.

Devadatta was among the nobles of the Shakya tribe who were converted when Shakyamuni visited Kapilavastu. A cousin of Shakyamuni and a brother of the famous disciple Ananda, Devadatta converted when he was still in his twenties and was thus about thirty years younger than Shakyamuni. Far from being a troublemaker, he was instrumental, along with the other young nobles of the Shakya clan, in instilling vigor into the Order.

The first indications of his treachery came to light immediately after a visit made to the region of Kaushambi to the west. Shakyamuni seems to have made a number of journeys to Kaushambi, but this particular one took place about thirty years after his enlightenment. At this time, Devadatta, who had previously been guileless and single-minded in his religious practice, became consumed by thoughts of wealth and fame. Such ambitions have often corrupted the minds of those with an otherwise devout disposition, and Devadatta, in spite of his earlier sincerity, proved to be no exception. Filled with dreams of winning the leadership of the Order away from Shakyamuni, he began by approaching Ajatashatru, the son of King Bimbisara of Magadha.

Devadatta knew that Prince Ajatashatru was jealous of the prestige his father enjoyed and disgruntled because his father would not relinquish the throne to him, and Devadatta skillfully played upon the prince's discontent and frustration until he had worked his way into the young man's confidence. The prince in turn presented various gifts to Devadatta, which aroused the envy of the other members of the Order. Shakyamuni thereupon admonished his disciples for their pettiness. Reminding them that the passion for fame and wealth ran counter to the Buddhist spirit, he predicted that the prince's gifts and honors would eventually be the ruin of Devadatta.

Shakyamuni had by this time no doubt seen through Devadatta's ambitions. At first merely envious of the universal adulation that Shakyamuni enjoyed from the people around him, Devadatta had become increasingly jealous of the Buddha and convinced that he himself should take over the leadership of the Order. He even went so far as to ask Shakyamuni in the presence of the other disciples to retire and place the Buddhist Order in his charge. Shakyamuni reproached him stiffly, saying that this was out of the question; he would not entrust the leadership of the Order even to such outstanding disciples as Shariputra and Maudgalyayana, much less to a person like Devadatta. This was a great blow to the pride of the ambitious Devadatta. He was especially hurt because Shakyamuni had told him that Shariputra and Maudgalyayana were like "blazing torches," whereas his own mediocre intelligence shed "even less light than a night lamp." Having thus failed to acquire the position he coveted, he seems to have lost all sense of reason and human decency and began to hatch schemes to do away with Shakyamuni.

First, Devadatta goaded Prince Ajatashatru into rebelling against his father, who was a patron and faithful follower of Shakyamuni. Convinced that his father's longevity would bar him from the throne forever, the prince had the old king imprisoned and starved to death, taking his place as ruler of Magadha. According to a different version of the tale, the king discovered the conspiracy beforehand but, seeing how anxious his son was to reign, voluntarily relinquished the throne to him. In any event, through Devadatta's machinations, Ajatashatru became the king of Magadha and Devadatta's enthusiastic patron and supporter.

Devadatta's next step was to plot an attack on Shakyamuni. He persuaded the king to hire assassins to kill Shakyamuni, but when the assassins saw the Buddha, they fell at his feet in worship. Devadatta grew bolder and, choosing a time when Shakyamuni was at Mount Gridhrakuta (also known as Vulture or Eagle Peak), hurled a rock at him from the mountaintop. Only a fragment of the rock struck Shakyamuni, injuring him slightly in the foot, but the incident is significant as the first attempt made by Devadatta in person to take the Buddha's life.

Another legend relates that Devadatta loosed a mad elephant in the street where Shakyamuni was begging alms, but the elephant, like the hired assassins, was awestruck and humbled by the Buddha's presence and did him no harm.

Devadatta's gravest offense, however, is said to have been his attempt to sow dissension in the Order, which up until this time had enjoyed great harmony and unity of purpose. Devadatta advocated monastic rules even stricter than those upheld by Shakyamuni and so tried to make himself appear superior to the Buddha. There are some discrepancies depending upon the source, but the precepts Devadatta advocated are more or less as follows: (1) Practitioners should dwell in the woods away from villages or towns; those who enter villages or towns are committing an offense. (2) Practitioners should live on alms alone; those who accept invitations to banquets are committing an offense. (3) Practitioners should dress in rags; those who accept donated robes are committing an offense. (4) Practitioners should dwell under trees and not under a roof; those who go near a roofed abode are committing an offense. (5) Practitioners should not eat the flesh of animals or fish; those who break this precept are committing an offense

The fact that Devadatta could come forward with these proposals is ample indication that, as we have said above, the Buddhist Order did not practice or condone extreme austerities or forms of discipline. Specifically, the first proposal was intended as an indirect criticism of the Order for using the Jetavana Monastery, the Bamboo Grove Monastery, and similar establishments as headquarters and retreats during the rainy season, while the second expressed disapproval of the considerable donations that were often presented to the Order by wealthy and influential believers as Shakyamuni's fame spread among the populace.

As the proposals indicate, Devadatta, his earlier schemes having failed, was attempting to create dissension within the Order by pretending to be in favor of far greater austerities than had been practiced heretofore and by urging the monks and nuns to support his suggestions.

Devadatta's was a very clever plot. As Devadatta had foreseen, Shakyamuni would not countenance the enforcement of such strict rules and abruptly dismissed the proposals. Devadatta, feigning outrage, then called upon the other members of the Order to support him. Attracted to the principles of purity and austerity that he upheld, we are told, about five hundred recently ordained members left the Order and followed Devadatta to Mount Gayashirsha. This was the first schism to occur in the history of the Buddhist Order.

The moral of this episode would seem to be that ambitious men, by proclaiming high-sounding principles and appearing to be purer in faith than those around them, are capable of deceiving and leading others astray. It points up more than ever the truism that one cannot judge a man on the basis of his words alone. It is unfortunate that in the history of humankind, appeals for greater purity and fidelity to higher principles should so often be employed by hypocritical people as tools to mislead others and advance their own schemes.

By cleverly exploiting people's psychological weaknesses, Devadatta brought about a temporary schism within the Order. Shakyamuni, however, dispatched his most trusted disciples, Shariputra and Maudgalyayana, to preach to the dissidents, and the five hundred monks, seeing through Devadatta's pretensions, soon returned to the fold. According to legend, when Devadatta learned of this, he was so enraged that he coughed up blood and died not long afterward.

Because of the enormity of his deeds and the fact that in the end he failed so completely, the subject of Devadatta's revolt is treated at length in the Buddhist scriptures. In the "Devadatta" chapter of the Lotus Sutra, however, Shakyamuni foretells salvation and enlightenment for the reprobate, setting forth the doctrine that even the most evil of people can attain Buddhahood.

In the Lotus Sutra, Devadatta the historical personage is used to typify what is in fact a universal tendency within human beings. The ambition and the passion for honor and wealth that drove Devadatta to his acts of evil lurk in our own minds as well, an inherent part of human nature. Blinded by ambition, we too are in danger of losing self-control and a proper perspective. We may even attempt to satisfy our desires through deceit or evildoing. At the same time the Lotus Sutra teaches us that we too are certain to achieve Buddhahood if we can learn to contemplate and understand our own natures and devote ourselves wholeheartedly to the highest objectives.

The problem before us is how to keep in check the Devadatta who inhabits the deep recesses of our mind and instead awaken the Buddhahood inherent in us. This is the most essential point in Buddhist practice, and it is through the process of striving to solve this problem that we develop true strength of character. For this reason, the Deva-datta episode is of great significance to us today, offering an opportunity to think deeply about our own faith and manner of life.

As for Devadatta's royal patron King Ajatashatru, he is said to have fallen gravely ill as a result of the evil deeds that he committed. He repented and became a devout Buddhist. After Shakyamuni's death, he continued to work diligently for the propagation of the faith. He is well known in later times for his part in helping to collect and put in order the Buddhist scriptures.

THE ENTRY INTO NIRVANA

8

THE SAD EVENTS OF SHAKYAMUNI'S CLOSING YEARS

The circumstances surrounding Shakyamuni's death, or, more properly speaking, his entry into nirvana, are recounted at length in the Mahaparinirvana Sutra [Great Complete Nirvana Sutra]. Unlike the accounts of the attainment of enlightenment, which are presented mostly in the form of Shakyamuni's own reminiscences, the entry into nirvana is recorded in the form of recollections by his disciples.

According to this account, Shakyamuni, accompanied by Ananda and some five hundred other followers, left Eagle Peak on the outskirts of Rajagriha and journeyed northward. He died in a grove of sal trees near the city of Kushinagara in the land of the Mallas. The sutra covers some six months before and after this event, including the funeral, cremation of the body, and division of the ashes among the mourners. But before the last journey, two events occurred in rapid succession that caused great grief for Shakyamuni. First were the deaths of his two most trusted disciples, Shariputra and Maudgalyayana; second was the downfall of the Shakya tribe.

Shariputra and Maudgalyayana constituted the very pillars of the Order. As we have noted earlier, they were singled out as being "foremost in wisdom" and "foremost in transcendental powers," respectively, and were also renowned for the deep and lasting friendship that existed between them. So important and influential were they that

one account preserved by writers of the Jain religion actually identi-
fies Shariputra rather than Shakyamuni as the leader of the Buddhist
Order.

During Shakyamuni's later years, these two disciples preached and
expounded sutras in their master's stead, and when the Order faced
its first major crisis over the schism created by Devadatta, it was these
two who were sent by Shakyamuni to win back the dissenting monks.
Though Shakyamuni never clearly indicated who his successor was to
be, he must have looked upon Shariputra and Maudgalyayana as promising candidates for the role, since they were universally recognized
both for their wisdom and their diligence in religious practice.

To Shakyamuni's great sorrow, however, both of these remarkable
men preceded him in death. Shariputra contracted an illness and died
at his native village of Nalaka; Maudgalyayana is said to have been killed
by a Brahman while he was wandering about begging alms. One senses
a mysterious link between the fates of the two close friends, since they
died at almost the same time. An account of how grieved Shakyamuni
was by the loss of his two greatest disciples is recorded in one of the
scriptures, "Since Shariputra and Maudgalyayana died, this gathering
seems empty to me!"

Sensing his own impending death, Shakyamuni must have been
unbearably saddened by the event, though so great and encompassing
was his affection for his disciples that one feels he might have spoken
the same words upon the death of anyone of them. Nevertheless, he
did not allow the sad occurrence to overwhelm him but, surmounting
his grief, put forth greater efforts than ever for the growth and development of the Buddhist Order. In one scripture, he admonishes his disciples for their despondency over the loss of Shariputra, saying: "What is
there for you to grieve over? What have you lost as a result of Shariputra's death?"

A great many things would happen to the Order in the future, for
the essence of this world is impermanence and perpetual change. The

important thing, Shakyamuni understood, was to establish a solid and indestructible strength of character that would enable each person to understand the true nature of change and survive it. Herein lies the essence of Buddhism, and Shakyamuni expected his followers, as men and women who had pledged to propagate and protect the Buddhist faith, to understand this. This, I believe, is what he had in mind when he admonished his disciples for grieving over the death of Shariputra. He knew, too, that the day was not far off when they would have to cope with the grief of his own passing.

At approximately the same time as the death of his two leading disciples, Shakyamuni received word of the downfall of the Shakya clan. His life, which had been beset with difficulties from the time of his enlightenment, continued to be stormy even during these last years.

It was Virudhaka, the new ruler of Kosala, who attacked and destroyed the Shakyas. The son of King Prasenajit, he seized the throne at a time when his father was absent on a visit to the Shakya state. The old king was then eighty years of age. Thus the two royal patrons of Buddhism, Prasenajit and Bimbisara, both met with the same fate in their old age. Prasenajit set out for Rajagriha to seek assistance from Ajatashatru, the ruler of Magadha, but died on the way.

There is a well-known story behind Virudhaka's attack on the Shakyas. The state of Kosala had only recently risen to prominence under the leadership of King Prasenajit. The king, hoping to increase the prestige of his royal family, decided that he would like a bride from the Shakya clan, which was noted for its ancient and noble lineage and its patronage of learning.

The Shakyas were too proud simply to hand over one of the royal princesses to a man whom they regarded as an upstart. On the other hand, they were a vassal kingdom under the control of the far more powerful Kosala and therefore were in no position to ignore the request entirely. The king of the Shakyas thereupon devised a scheme whereby, rather than a full-blooded princess, he passed off on King Prasenajit a girl who had been born to him by a maidservant. King Prasenajit married the girl, and soon she bore him a son, who was none other than Virudhaka.

Virudhaka was educated in the kingdom of the Shakyas, where he underwent training in the military arts. Coarse and violent by temperament and with a streak of brutality in his nature, he was disliked by the Shakyas, who looked on him with contempt and openly humiliated him for his lowly birth on his mother's side. He must have been burning with the desire to exact revenge, for no sooner had he seized the throne from his father than he marched against the Shakya kingdom at the head of a vast army.

According to some sources, he was met on the occasion of this first attack by Shakyamuni, who happened to be visiting his home at the time, and was persuaded by the Buddha to withdraw his army.

Virudhaka invaded the vassal kingdom several more times but was restrained each time by Shakyamuni. The latter, however, seems eventually to have realized that his country was doomed to destruction and to have set off on the next stage of his preaching tour. After his departure, the vengeful king returned once more and annihilated the little state of the Shakyas.

Looking back on these events, we note that a certain forlorn aura seems to have surrounded Shakyamuni in his last years. The essential impermanence of the phenomenal world, which he had come to understand through his enlightenment and had attempted to teach to others, was dramatically demonstrated in one event after another. Nevertheless, or perhaps because of such events, he continued his efforts to awaken people to the true nature of reality, preaching the Law with unflagging energy until the time of his death.

~

THE LAST JOURNEY

After the fall of the Shakyas, Shakyamuni returned to Rajagriha and stayed there for some time. When in Rajagriha, he customarily made his headquarters in the Bamboo Grove Monastery, but when it was not the rainy season he also frequently went to Eagle Peak, situated on the outskirts of the city. According to various sources, it was one of his favorite spots in Magadha, and he often climbed it in the company of his numerous disciples.

Eagle Peak is not a high mountain and therefore was easy enough to ascend. It consists mostly of rock and takes its name from a formation at the top that is said to resemble a vulture or eagle. There is a hot spring nearby, which is rare in India, and the mountaintop commands a sweeping view of the dense forests below. It must have been an ideal spot for meditation, and one can also imagine that Shakyamuni utilized his visits there to preach to his disciples. It was at Eagle Peak that he is said to have preached the Lotus Sutra. And it was from Eagle Peak that he set off on what was to be his last journey.

Before embarking on that journey, Shakyamuni rested for a while. He was by this time eighty years old, but he did not allow age to deter him from preaching, a fact that has been an inspiration to his followers down through the ages. Until the last moment of his life, he labored to spread the truth for the salvation of all humankind. And because of his devotion and purity of purpose, he remained youthful and vigorous in spirit.

Physically, however, Shakyamuni had by this time grown quite thin and weak, as he himself was well aware. He told Ananda, who accompanied him on his final journey: "I am old now, Ananda; I have grown feeble. My journey nears its end, and I have reached my sum of days, for I am eighty years old. Just as a worn-out cart can move only if it is tied with thongs, so my body functions only with the help of thongs."

Shakyamuni's last journey is said to have ended in Kushinagara, but after examining the map I am inclined to think that, having crossed the Ganges, he was actually on his way to Kapilavastu, farther to the north. Possibly he wanted to set foot on his native soil once more before he died. But death overtook him while he was still on the way.

From Eagle Peak he journeyed to the village of Patali, where he crossed the Ganges and entered the land of the Vrijis. Along the way, he preached to various people, as was his custom, and many are reported to have been moved and converted to the faith. A number of the sermons that he delivered at this time are recorded in the scriptures.

There is a famous anecdote concerning one such sermon that Shakyamuni preached in a forest on the outskirts of Vaishali, the capital of Vriji. This forest was owned by a courtesan named Ambapali, who was a convert to Buddhism. Hearing that Shakyamuni had come to her forest, she hurried to the spot and listened to his sermon. Profoundly moved, when it was over she invited him to dinner. He accepted, treating her with the same respect as the noblemen who had likewise come to hear him. Later some of the noblemen also invited him to dinner, but Shakyamuni courteously refused, saying that he had a previous engagement with Ambapali. This episode illustrates first of all the impartiality with which Shakyamuni treated men and women of all social classes, but it also shows that he was the kind of person who respected the ordinary rules of social behavior.

Keeping his promise to Ambapali, Shakyamuni went the following day to her house for dinner and, after dinner, preached the Law to her. She was deeply moved, and one legend says that she donated her forest and mansion to the Order. Following this incident, Shakyamuni, accompanied by Ananda, went into retreat at a place called Beluva for the duration of the monsoon season, while the other disciples dispersed, seeking refuge elsewhere.

During this last retreat, Shakyamuni became seriously ill. The exact nature of the illness is not known, but it is said to have caused him considerable pain. By sheer force of will, however, he eventually overcame it. Ananda naturally was alarmed but did not know what steps to take to alleviate his master's illness. Some sources say that he was not unduly worried about the outcome of the illness, however, because he felt certain that Shakyamuni would not pass away until he had left his instructions concerning the Order. From this, one can see that Shakyamuni's disciples were entirely dependent upon him and content merely to carry out his orders.

Observing this attitude of utter dependence in Ananda and aware that his end was approaching, Shakyamuni is said to have spoken to his disciple in these words: "What does the Order expect of me, Ananda? I have taught the Law without making any distinction between exoteric and esoteric doctrines. With the All-Awakened One, there is no such thing as the closed fist of the teacher who hides some things from his disciples."

He was saying that he had already taught his followers all there was to know about the Law, and that it was useless for them to expect any more from him. From now on, they had only to abide by the Law and spread it. As to his attitude toward the Order, he went on to say, "If anyone thinks, 'I will lead the *sangha*,' or 'The *sangha* depends on me,' he is the one who should lay down instructions for the *bhikkhus*. However, the Tathagata does not think, 'It is I who will lead the *sangha*,' or 'The *bhikkhus* depend on me.'"

In his own view, Shakyamuni was not the leader of the Order but in fact merely one of its members, seeking the truth like all the rest. These words indicate Shakyamuni's humility and also serve to sum up his whole life. His attitude toward his disciples was that of a friend and comrade who, like them, was striving toward the same goal and acknowledged the same philosophy of life. With these words, he doubtless wished to dispel the deep feeling of dependence that Ananda and the other disciples held toward him. He was admonishing them to depend on the Law, not on Shakyamuni.

Later, when he realized that he was about to die, Shakyamuni left the following instructions concerning the Order and the conduct of the monks: "Therefore, you must be your own islands. Take the self as your refuge. Take refuge in nothing outside yourselves. Hold firm to the Law as an island, and do not seek refuge in anything besides yourselves." With these words, Shakyamuni aptly defined the basic spirit in which the monks should carry out their religious practice and assume responsibility for themselves. One tends to think of the self as rather frail and unreliable, and it may seem surprising to find the Buddha laying such emphasis upon it. By "self" here, however, he does not mean the ordinary self that is subject to sudden changes through the influence of outside causes but the self that aspires to a state of permanence through the Law. Once such a self is firmly established, then one of the fundamental objectives of Buddhism has been realized and the individual is free to devote the remainder of his or her time to the salvation of others and the perpetuation of the Law.

In Buddhism, dependence on others is not sought, and help from others is not awaited. The individual must establish a sound understanding, bright and clear as a mirror, and march forward solely accompanied by that understanding. The Law is the foundation upon which to build such a self. And the Law is inherent within the life of each and every individual; it does not exist outside the self. This, I believe, is what the founder of the Tiantai sect of Buddhism in China meant when, expounding on the fundamental principles of Buddhism, he spoke of "the teachings of the Buddha practiced within your mind."

In the final analysis, no religion places greater emphasis upon the dignity of the individual and one's subjective nature than Buddhism. This is the essential difference between Buddhism and most other religions. While most religions recognize the "absolute" as existing outside the self, Buddhism does not. In Buddhism the only absolute is the dharma, or Law of Life, which is nothing other than that which exists within the self. It remains only for the individual to realize this truth

THE ENTRY INTO NIRVANA ■ 133

and to draw out the dharma that is within. In other words, one transforms the present changeable self into the self as it should be, the self that is in perfect harmony with the Law. This humanism, which can also be called *human revolution*, constitutes the very essence of Buddhism.

~

CHUNDA THE BLACKSMITH

Shakyamuni spent the last monsoon season of his life at Beluva on the outskirts of Vaishali. Resting under a *chapala* tree one day after the rains had ended, he is said to have remarked, "This world is beautiful— it is a joy to live in it!"

We are always curious to know how the world appears to a person who is facing death. The well-known Japanese novelist Ryunosuke Akutagawa is said to have remarked just before committing suicide: "Nature seems to me more beautiful than ever. This is because I set eyes on it for the last time." Shakyamuni saw this same beauty about him, yet his words do not reveal the faintest trace of lingering attachment to the world. Rather they are expressive of a sense of contentment, of a life fulfilled. Shakyamuni was to die the serene, composed death of a true sage.

Leaving behind the beautiful region of Vaishali, Shakyamuni continued his journey northward with Ananda as his companion. After passing through a number of villages, where he taught the Law, he proceeded to a place called Pava. In this village, Shakyamuni and his followers stayed in a mango grove owned by a man named Chunda.

Though only a lowly blacksmith, Chunda unwittingly managed to involve himself in the Buddha's entry into nirvana. Welcoming Shakyamuni warmly, he listened to the master's sermons and asked questions, which the latter answered with care. Deeply moved, Chunda invited the Buddha and his disciples to dine at his house and, in a mood of joy and thanksgiving, had a special meal prepared for them, the main ingredient of which is said to have been some kind of mushroom. Shakyamuni graciously accepted his hospitality and talked with the blacksmith as courteously as he would with a prince or a Brahman. Unfortunately for Shakyamuni, who was already in a weakened condition, the meal proved to have dire consequences. After eating, Shakyamuni began to suffer violent pain and soon became seriously ill. The nature of the illness is not known but is presumed to have been dysentery, since it is recorded that it was accompanied by diarrhea and intestinal bleeding.

Ananda, in his distress, berated Chunda, but Shakyamuni restrained him and said that great rewards would go to the man for the meal that he had offered in all sincerity. Though the meal occasioned a recurrence of illness, this, as Shakyamuni realized, had nothing to do with the spirit of reverence and gratitude in which it had been prepared. Chunda was not to be blamed. Shakyamuni perceived that it was only human nature to want to condemn Chunda, so he took pains to point out the folly of such behavior.

~

PARINIRVANA

In spite of the severe pains that now beset him, Shakyamuni insisted upon continuing his preaching tour with Ananda by his side as usual. But by this time, he was too weakened by age and illness to proceed very far. His last stop was Kushinagara.

Kushinagara is situated southeast of Kapilavastu. Though still a long way away, Shakyamuni was drawing nearer to his home step by step, but the day came when he could go no farther. Upon reaching Kushinagara, he retired to a grove of sal trees and had a couch spread for him beneath the trees. Sal trees are said to have grown in great numbers in the Kushinagara area in ancient times and are still to be found there today.

Resting on the couch that Ananda prepared for him, Shakyamuni realized clearly that death was approaching, and he asked Ananda to inform the people of the Malla tribe living in the town of Kushinagara that the Buddha was about to enter nirvana. The Mallas came at once to pay homage. Among them was an ascetic who asked to be brought into the presence of the Buddha so that he might question him about the Law. Ananda, concerned over his master's condition, tried to deny the request, and an argument between them ensued. Overhearing it, Shakyamuni asked the ascetic to approach his bedside and, after answering his questions on the Law, accepted him into the Order.

Then Shakyamuni addressed the monks gathered around his couch, saying: "Decay is inherent in all composite things. Work out your own salvation with diligence." These are reported to be his last words. Toward midnight of the same day, the event known in Buddhist terminology as the *parinirvana*, or "final nirvana," took place. In Japan, February 15 is celebrated as the anniversary of Shakyamuni's entry into nirvana, calculated on the basis of the legend relating that, like his enlightenment, it took place at the end of the night of the full moon of Vaishakha.

One of the scriptures gives the following dramatic account of the scene: "The sal trees burst into full bloom out of season, bent down over the Tathagata, and showered the body with their flowers, as if to do the Buddha supreme honor. There were heavenly flowers that rained down and scattered over the Tathagata as if to do the Buddha supreme honor.... And the world was like a mountain whose summit has been shattered by a thunderbolt; it was like the sky without the moon."

Whatever may have occurred, we may be certain that it was a fitting close to a life that had been characterized throughout by a striving for gentleness, harmony, serenity, and peace. A funeral pyre was built by the grieving disciples, and the body of the Buddha was cremated seven days after his death. His ashes, which came to be looked upon as sacred relics, were divided among the representatives of various tribal groups and King Ajatashatru of Magadha.

The death of a truly great man often marks the beginning rather than the end of an era in terms of the progress of the human spirit. The difference lies in whether that man lived essentially for his own glory alone or devoted his life to the pursuit of the eternal principles of truth and to the true happiness of all humankind. Shakyamuni belonged to the latter category, and his message, far from dying with him, was transmitted by his followers to the people of later ages, initiating a new era in the spiritual history of humanity not only in the country of his birth but throughout the Asian continent.

Though the history of Buddhism had only just begun, I will end this account where the life of its founder ends.

GLOSSARY

Agama sutras A group of sutras containing Shakyamuni's earlier teachings. *Agama* means "teachings handed down by tradition." The Chinese Agama sutras comprise four groups, each containing a number of sutras. The four groups, or the four Agama sutras, as they are commonly known, are the Long Agama Sutra, the Medium-Length Agama Sutra, the Miscellaneous Agama Sutra, and the Increasing by One Agama Sutra.

Agni Brahmanic god of fire.

Ajatashatru King of Magadha and son of King Bimbisara.

Ajita Kesakambala One of the six non-Buddhist teachers.

Alara Kalama A hermit-sage and master of yogic meditation who lived near Rajagriha. He was the first teacher under whom Shakyamuni studied and practiced after renouncing the secular world.

Ambapali Courtesan who, upon hearing the teachings of Shakyamuni, donated her forest of mango trees to the Buddhist Order (Ambapali Garden).

Ananda Cousin of Shakyamuni and one of Shakyamuni's ten major disciples. Also, the brother of Devadatta.

Anathapindada *See* Sudatta.

Anga One of the sixteen great states in ancient India.

Angulimala Brigand who became a disciple of Shakyamuni. *Angulimala* means "necklace of fingers," a name said to derive from a necklace he wore made of the severed fingers of those he had murdered.

Aniruddha A cousin of Shakyamuni and one of the ten major disciples.

anuttara-samyak-sambodhi "Supreme perfect enlightenment," the unsurpassed enlightenment of a Buddha. *Anuttara* means supreme, highest, incomparable, unsurpassed, or peerless. *Samyak* means right, correct, true, accurate, complete, or perfect, and *sambodhi* means enlightenment.

Aranyakas "Forest Treatises," Brahmanic works produced around 600 BCE.

arhat One who has attained the highest of the four stages that voice-hearers aim to achieve through the practice of Hinayana teachings; that is, the highest stage of Hinayana enlightenment. *Arhat* means one worthy of respect.

Ashoka (r. c. 268–232 BCE) Buddhist ruler, third monarch of the Maurya dynasty and the first king to unify India.

Ashvaghosha A Mahayana scholar and poet from Shravasti in India who lived from the first through the second century. According to another account, he was from Shaketa in India. *Ashva* means horse, and *ghosha*, cry or sound.

Ashvajit One of the early disciples of Shakyamuni.

Asita A seer of Kapilavastu in northern India.

asura A type of contentious and belligerent demon in Indian mythology.

atman The Self or soul in Brahmanic thought

Avanti An ancient kingdom of west-central India. Its capital was Ujjayini.

bhikkhu (Pali) "One who begs for food"; Buddhist monk.

bhikkhuni (Pali) Buddhist nun.

Bimbisara King of Magadha and a follower of Shakyamuni.

bodhisattva One who aspires to enlightenment, or Buddhahood. *Bodhi* means enlightenment, and *sattva*, a living being.

bodhi tree The pipal tree at Buddhagaya, India, under which Shakyamuni attained enlightenment.

Brahma A god said to rule over the Earth. In Indian mythology, he was regarded as the personification of the fundamental universal principle (Brahman), and he was incorporated into Buddhism as one of the two major tutelary gods, the other being Shakra.

brahmacharin Studenthood; the first of the four traditional Brahman periods of life.

Brahman The priestly class, the highest of the four castes in ancient India.

Buddha One enlightened to the eternal and ultimate truth that is the reality of all things, and who leads others to attain the same enlightenment.

Buddhagaya The place where Shakyamuni attained enlightenment under the *bodhi* tree. Today it is called Bodh Gaya or Buddh Gaya.

chakravartin Wheel-turning king; ideal rulers in Indian mythology. *Chakra* means wheel, and *vartin*, one who turns.

Chandaka A servant of Shakyamuni before he renounced secular life.

Chunda Blacksmith in Pava Village in northern India who offered Shakyamuni his last meal before his death.

Devadatta A cousin of Shakyamuni who, after Shakyamuni's enlightenment, first followed him as a disciple but later became his enemy.

dharma Dharma has a wide variety of meanings, such as law, truth, doctrine, the Buddha's teaching, decree, observances, conduct, duty, virtue, morality, religion, justice, nature, quality, character, character, characteristic, essence, elements of existence, and phenomena.

dhuta A discipline or ascetic practice to purify one's body and mind and remove one's desire for food, clothing, and shelter.

dhyana (Jpn *zen*) Meditation.

Eagle Peak A small mountain located northeast of Rajagriha, the capital of Magadha in ancient India (also known as Gridhrakuta, or Vulture Peak).

Flower Garland Sutra Also, Avatamsaka Sutra; the basic text of the Flower Garland school. According to this sutra, Shakyamuni expounded the teaching it contains immediately after he attained enlightenment under the *bodhi* tree in the kingdom of Magadha, India.

Gautama The family name of the historial Buddha, Shakyamuni.

Gaya Kashyapa One of three brothers in Uruvilva, India, who converted to Shakyamuni's teachings in his early days of preaching. His brothers are Uruvilva Kashyapa and Nadi Kashyapa.

ghat A broad flight of steps situated on an Indian riverbank that provides access to the water, especially for bathing.

grihastha Householder; second of the four traditional Brahman periods of life.

Ikshvaku "Sugar Cane King," legendary ancestor of the Puru tribe and of Shakyamuni.

Jatila Sect of Brahman ascetics.

Jeta Crown prince of Kosala.

Jetavana Monastery Monastery (*vihana*) in Shravasti, India, where Shakyamuni is said to have lived and taught during the rainy season for the last twenty-five years of his life. Sudatta built it as an offering on land provided by Prince Jeta.

Kanthaka Shakyamuni's horse.

Kapilavastu The ancient kingdom of the Shakya tribe; also a small state on the Indian Nepalese border.

karma Potentials in the inner, unconscious realm of life created through one's actions in the past or present that manifest themselves as various results in the present or future.

Kashi One of the sixteen great states of India in the sixth century BCE. Its capital was Varanasi.

Katyayana One of Shakyamuni's ten major disciples, he was known as "foremost in debate."

Kaundinya One of the five ascetics who heard Shakyamuni Buddha's first sermon and became his disciples.

Khema Consort of King Bimbisara who became a Buddhist nun.

Koliya Tribe in ancient India.

Kosala Kingdom in ancient India, in the eastern part of what is now Uttar Pradesh, India's northern state. Around the sixth century BCE, it was one of the sixteen great states in India and, along with Magadha, one of the two greatest powers in the subcontinent. The capital was Shravasti.

Kshatriya Comprised of nobles and warriors, this was the ruling class, the second highest of the four castes in ancient Indian Brahmanic society.

Kushinagara The capital city of Malla in northern India, one of the sixteen great states during Shakyamuni's lifetime. Shakyamuni died in a grove of sal trees in the northern part of Kushinagara.

Licchavi A tribe that dwelt north of the Ganges River. The Licchavis, with their capital at Vaishali, were rivals of the Magadha kingdom to the south.

Lumbini Gardens Birthplace of Shakyamuni; a grove in what is today the village of Rummindei just inside the southern border of Nepal.

Magadha The most powerful of the sixteen great states in ancient India. It covered an area south of the Ganges River in what is now the state of Behar in northeastern India. Its capital was Rajagriha.

Mahakashyapa Also known as Kashyapa. One of Shakyamuni's ten major disciples, he was known as "foremost in the ascetic practices" called *dhuta*.

Mahaparinirvana Sutra A reference to several Chinese translations of different texts; literally, Great Complete Nirvana Sutra.

Mahaprajapati Maternal aunt and foster mother of Shakyamuni.

Mahayana Buddhism "Buddhism of the Great Vehicle"; the Sanskrit *maha* means great, and *yana*, vehicle. Mahayana emphasizes altruistic practice—called the bodhisattva practice—as a means to attain enlightenment for oneself and help others attain it as well.

Makkhali Gosala One of the six non-Buddhist teachers.

Mara Devil; a personification of evil. The Sanskrit word *mara* also means killing, death, pestilence, or obstacles, and in China it was translated as "robber of life."

Maudgalyayana One of Shakyamuni's ten major disciples, he is known as "foremost in transcendental powers."

Maya The wife of King Shuddhodana and mother of Shakyamuni. She died seven days after giving birth to Shakyamuni.

Medium-Length Agama Sutra One of the four Agama sutras. It explains such basic doctrines as the four noble truths and the twelve-linked chain of causation.

Mrigara-matri Hall Buddhist establishment in Shravasti.

munda "Tonsured one," a term for Buddhist monks.

munja A kind of sedgelike grass.

Nadi Kashyapa One of three brothers in Uruvilva, India, who converted to Shakyamuni's teachings in his early days of preaching. His brothers are Uruvilva Kashyapa and Gaya Kashyapa.

Nagarjuna A Mahayana scholar of southern India thought to have lived between the years 150 and 250.

Nigantha Nataputta One of the six non-Buddhist teachers and founder of the Jain religion.

nirvana Enlightenment, the ultimate goal of Buddhist practice. The Sanskrit word *nirvana* means "blown out" and is variously translated as extinction, emancipation, cessation, quiescence, or non-birth.

Pakudha Kacchayana One of the six non-Buddhist teachers

parinirvana Complete nirvana. *Pari* means round, complete, or final. *Nirvana* refers to the death, or "passing into extinction," of a Buddha. Nirvana also means emancipation from delusion and suffering, or enlightenment.

Pava Village in northern India where Shakyamuni ate his last meal before his death.

Praising the Buddha's Deeds An epic written by Ashvaghosha who lived in India from the first through the second century. It recounts the life of Shakyamuni from his birth to the distribution of his ashes after his death.

prajna The wisdom that perceives the true nature of all things. Because *prajna* leads to enlightenment, it is regarded as the mother or source of all Buddhas.

prajna-paramita The perfection of wisdom. One of the six paramitas. *Prajna* means wisdom that penetrates the essential nature of all things. *Paramita* means perfection.

Prasenajit King of Kosala and a follower of Shakyamuni.

pratitya-samutpada Dependent origination; a Buddhist doctrine expressing the interdependence of all things.

pratyekabuddha Cause-awakened one; one who perceives the twelve-linked chain of causation, or the truth of causal relationship; the eighth of the Ten Worlds, or world of realization.

Purana Kassapa One of the six non-Buddhist teachers.

Purna One of Shakyamuni's ten major disciples; known as "foremost in preaching the Law."

Rahula Son of Shakyamuni and one of his ten major disciples; known as "foremost in inconspicuous practice."

Rajagriha Capital of the kingdom of Magadha.

Shaketa City in Kosala, one of the sixteen great states of ancient India.

samadhi A state of intense concentration of mind, or meditation, said to produce inner serenity; translated as meditation, contemplation, or concentration.

samsara Transmigration; the cycle of birth and death that ordinary people undergo in the world of illusion and suffering.

sangha The Buddhist Order, or the community of Buddhist believers. One of the three treasures of Buddhism, the other two being the Buddha and his teachings.

Sanjaya Belatthiputta One of the six non-Buddhist teachers.

sannyasin Homeless wanderer; last of the four traditional Brahman periods of life.

Saptaparna-guha Cave of the Seven Leaves; the site where the First Buddhist Council for the compilation of Shakyamuni's teachings was held shortly after his death with the support of Ajatashatru, the king of Magadha in India.

Sarnath Site near Varanasi where Shakyamuni preached his first sermon to the five ascetics.

Shravasti Capital of Kosala.

Shakya A tribe that lived in the area along the modern Indian-Nepalese border in the southern foothills of the Himalayas. Shakyamuni came from this tribe.

Shakyamuni "Sage of the Shakyas"; the founder of Buddhism.

Shariputra One of Shakyamuni's ten major disciples; known as "foremost in wisdom."

shramana A seeker of the way. The word originally referred to any ascetic, recluse, mendicant, or other religious practitioner who renounced secular life and left home to seek the truth.

shreshthin Wealthy merchants or bankers.

Shuddhodana A king of Kapilavastu and the father of Shakyamuni.

Shudra Lowest of the four classes of Brahmanic society.

shunyata Non-substantiality; a fundamental Buddhist concept, also translated as emptiness, void, latency, or relativity.

Subhuti One of the ten major disciples of Shakyamuni, he was known as "foremost in understanding the doctrine of non-substantiality."

Sudatta A merchant of Shravasti and a lay patron of Shakyamuni; also called Anathapindada, "Supplier of the Needy."

Sujata A girl who offered food to Shakyamuni before he entered meditation to attain enlightenment.

tapas Literally, "heat"; ascetic practices.

tathagata The Thus Come One, an honorable title of a Buddha.

Theravada "Teaching of the Elders"; one of the two schools formed by the first schism in the Buddhist Order that took place about one hundred years after Shakyamuni's death. The other is the Mahasamghika school.

Treatise on the Middle Way One of Nagarjuna's principal works.

Uddaka Ramaputta A hermit and master of yogic meditation who lived in a forest near Rajagriha, the capital of Magadha. After Shakyamuni renounced the world to lead a religious life, Uddaka Ramaputta became his second teacher.

Upali One of Shakyamuni's ten major disciples; known as "foremost in observing the precepts."

Upanishads Brahmanic philosophical texts.

upasaka Buddhist laymen.

upasika Buddhist laywomen.

Uruvilva A village near Gaya in Magadha.

Uruvilva Kashyapa One of three brothers in Uruvilva, India, who converted to Shakyamuni's teachings in his early days of preaching. His brothers are Gaya Kashyapa and Nadi Kashyapa.

Utpalavarna A nun of Shakyamuni's Order.

vaipulya Great extension, development, largeness, or thickness, indicating a sutra of great breadth or scope; also "correct and equal." The third of the five periods of Shakyamuni's preaching, according to the Tiantai classification.

Vaishakha One of the twelve months of the lunar year in ancient India.

Vaishali Capital city of the Licchavi tribe.

Vaishya Merchant class, third of the four classes of Brahmanic society

Vriji One of the sixteen great states of ancient India.

vanaprastha Forest hermit; third of the four traditional Brahman periods of life

Varanasi A city on the left bank of the Ganges River in northern India; capital of the ancient kingdom of Kashi.

Vatsa One of the sixteen great states in ancient India; located south of the Gange River in what is today the Indian state of Uttar Pradesh. Its capital was Kaushambi.

Vedas Literally, "knowledge." Any of four canonical collections of hymns, prayers, and liturgical formulas that comprise the earliest Hindu sacred writings.

vihana Monastery.

vimukti Emancipation.

vinaya The rules of discipline for monks and nuns.

Vindhya Mountain range in central India.

Virudhaka King of Kosala and son of King Prasenajit.

Vishakha Woman who donated Mrigara-matri Hall to Shakyamuni.

voice-hearer Shakyamuni's disciples who heard his preaching and strove to attain enlightenment. *Shravaka*, or "one who hears the voice," in Shakyamuni's time referred to his disciples, both monks and laymen.

Xuanzang (600–664) Chinese priest and translator known for his travels through central Asian and India.

Yashas The son of a wealthy merchant in Varanasi, India, Yashas was Shakyamuni's sixth convert and the first after the conversion of the five ascetics.

Yashodhara Wife of Shakyamuni and mother of Rahula.

INDEX

Western Regions of the Great Tang
    Dynasty), 5
death, Shakyamuni's realization of, 10
Deer Park, 72. *See also* Sarnath
Deer Park Monastery, 115
demons, location of, 58
dependence, in Buddhism, 132
dependent origination, doctrine of,
    65–66
Descartes, enlightenment of, 60
destiny, changing, 61
Deutero-Isaiah, 35
Devadatta, 13, 100–01, 103–04, 110;
    Buddhist Order, role in, 119; con-
    duct of, 102; corruption of, 119–20;
    death of, 123; hurt Shakyamuni,
    schemes to, 121; hypocritical nature
    of, 121–23; monastic rules of, 121–22;
    Shakyamuni censures, 120; Shakya-
    muni describes the intelligence of, as
    "even less light than a night lamp,"
    120
"Devadatta" chapter (Lotus Sutra), 123
Dharmachakra-pravartana Sutra, 49
dhuta (mild ascetic precepts), and
    Shakyamuni, 93

Eagle Peak (Gridhrakuta), 121, 125;
    Shakyamuni and, 129
Eastern civilization, reason for the dom-
    inance of the Western civilization
    over, 42
ego, 50–51. *See also* self-denial
eightfold path, 74
emancipation, 42
enlightenment, 59; attaining great,
    57; obstacle to, 56; *see also* Mara
    (devil king); scriptural accounts
    of Shakyamuni's, 65–66; *see also*
    anuttara-samyak-sambodhi; true,
    44, 48

fame, 120
first great pivotal era, 35

Flower Garland Sutra, 75
four devils, 56
four noble truths, 74
four stages of meditation, Shakyamuni
    masters, 62
freedom, in different civilizations, 42

Ganges River, 45
Gautama Buddha, 4. *See also* Shakya-
    muni; Theravada Buddhism
Gautama Shramana, 31. *See also*
    Shakyamuni
Gayashirsha, Mount, 122
gedatsu. See emancipation
goma jodo (conquering Mara and attain-
    ing Buddhahood). *See* Mara (devil
    king)
Gosala, Makkhali, 31; doctrine of, 33

hedonism, 49–50
hermit-sage, in India, 40–41
human beings, Shakyamuni's view of,
    117, 119; understanding another, x
humanism, in Buddhism, 132
humanity, ignorance of the world
    of, 64
human revolution, 51; in Buddhism, 132
husband, Shakyamuni states the duties
    of, 117

ideals, of Indian young men, 18
ignorance, 66–67; life of, 64
Ikshvaku (Sugar Cane King), 7
India, four classes of, 26–27; nature of
    people of, 3; records keeping of his-
    torical events in, ix, 2
Indonesia, 4

Jainism, fasting in, 47; origin of, 31;
    teachings of, 50
Jains, 25
Jaspers, Karl, 35
Jesus Christ, enlightenment of, 60
Jeta, Prince, 98